PRAISE

Recently, denominational executive Ruth Fletcher and her pastor husband Ron had a 3 month sabbatical. Instead of going to Europe or hiking Glacier National Park, they took a road trip across the United States visiting "transforming congregations." *Thrive* is the result of that road trip, and a lifetime of pastoral experience.

Fletcher begins with listing "changing conditions" that have had profound impact on how mainline churches respond to society today. They include globalization, interdependence, dispersed power, racial and religious diversity, evolving complexity, new ethical questions, the growing gap between rich and poor, and the end of non-renewable planetary resources.

The bulk of the book is her engaging description of twelve "spiritual habits" she has identified in transforming congregations. For each of the twelve habits—praying, waking up, growing, aligning, engaging, testifying, welcoming, questioning, building capacity, giving thanks, collaborating, and choosing—she tells the story of a congregation finding its vocation through the spiritual practice, whether or not they have identified it.

Thrive is well-researched, ecumenically accessible, and practical. By focusing on the spiritual habits she has observed in transforming congregations, Fletcher describes rather than prescribes. There are no easy answers in this book, only stories of hope and hard work.

Bishop Jessica Crist
Montana Synod, Evangelical Lutheran Church in America

In this clear, concise and hope-filled book Ruth Fletcher offers substantive help and direction to congregational leaders and pastors alike. Grounded in her years of experience in a wide variety of church settings, her faithful observation of human life and her deep love of God, Ruth tells us stories of transformation that arise like green shoots from the most unexpected and unlikely of places. This book is a gem and I look forward to sharing it with my leadership team.

Rev. Laurie Rudel
Pastor, Queen Anne Christian Church
Seattle, Washington

That transformation is a spiritual process is well known. What exactly that means is less well understood. Ruth Fletcher fills the gap with this manual on congregational spiritual life. The pattern of spiritual habits she describes provides markers for congregations making their way through the lightly charted territory of transformation and mission in the 21ˢᵗ century. *Thrive* is a welcome and needed addition to the literature of congregational transformation.

Dr. Sharon Watkins
General Minister and President
Christian Church (Disciples of Christ)

THRIVE

SPIRITUAL HABITS OF TRANSFORMING CONGREGATIONS

RUTH A. FLETCHER

Energion Publications
Gonzalez, FL
2015

Cover Image: © Yewkeo | Dreamstime.com - Vision Space Photo
(Dreamstime.com ID 4654406

ISBN10: 1-63199-207-4
ISBN13: 978-1-63199-207-0
Library of Congress Control Number: 2015946449

Energion Publications
P. O. Box 841
Gonzalez, FL 32560
850-525-3916

energion.com
pubs@energion.com

To Ron,
who shares the journey with me

PREFACE

A blizzard swirled around me as I drove from Great Falls, Montana to Kalispell one evening. Snow pelted the windshield. I clenched the steering wheel and slowed to a crawl. I could not distinguish the sky from the ground. I wanted to pull over and wait for the storm to clear, but where was the edge of the road? If I stopped, another car might come up from behind and hit me. I had to keep moving, but how? I could not see the way forward.

Then, all of a sudden, a tiny spot of light appeared just ahead on the right. As I crept along, I spotted another, then another—reflectors catching my headlights. During other trips on that road in daylight hours they had been invisible to me, but now they stood out against the white of everything else, marking the path and lighting the way. As I passed one reflector, I scanned for the next, and eventually it emerged. It took a long time, but by traveling from marker to marker, I navigated the whole distance and arrived safely at a place where I could spend the night.

For the last fifty years, historic Protestant churches have been lost in a disorienting white-out caused by the massive cultural shifts taking place around them. Many congregations identifying with the Evangelical Lutherans, Presbyterians, United Methodists, Episcopalians, American Baptists, Disciples of Christ, and the United Church of Christ have not been able to see the way forward. Their numbers have continued to shrink while the median age of members has increased. Each year, their boards and councils have made cuts to mission giving as it has become harder to pay the minister, to make building repairs, and to come up with money for the heating bills.

But recently, a few churches have begun to emerge as "transforming congregations"—communities of faith which change themselves in order to change the world. Those congregations hold in common twelve spiritual habits that shine like reflectors in a blizzard. Those spiritual habits are learned behaviors that connect those churches with the way of life practiced by Jesus, with the sacred Spirit, and with the needs and gifts of their neighbors. Together they form the character of transforming congregations, shape the decisions they make together, and deepen the wisdom by which they navigate life's journey.

Trinity is one of those congregations. The church building sits in the middle of an urban neighborhood where second-generation German and first-generation Hispanic immigrants live side by side. Inside, the sanctuary is filled with color, life, and joy. Children's artwork adorns the walls. The sound of lively conversation and laughter fills the air between services.

The church is clear about its purpose. A description of its vision statement appears in every worship bulletin: "Called by God to Share Broken Bread and the Gospel with Our Neighbors." The values of community, grace, and justice written in bold block letters form the center of a collage on the church's brochure.

On Sunday morning, the congregation offers three worship services—one traditional service, one service designed for young children and their families, and one service conducted in Spanish. The music in those services ranges from organ to guitar to children's action songs. During the week, the church hosts a children's choir, a multi-cultural adult choir, an after-school homework help program for children, a Latina support group, and classes in English as a second language.

In response to the disproportionate number of gay, lesbian, bi-sexual, and transgender youth living homeless in the city, the church also runs a shelter that provides safe space where those young people can sleep, eat, store belongings, receive counseling, and access social and health services. Trinity partners with another organization that refers youth for the shelter who are interested in or are actively seeking employment or schooling. The purpose of the program is to help those young people safely transition out of homelessness and grow into independent, positive, and productive adults. Over the last several decades, Trinity has gone from being a fearful enclave focused on its own survival to a courageous spiritual community reaching out to others.

The purpose of this book is to name the spiritual habits common to transforming congregations like Trinity. It is written to embolden those historic Protestant churches that are just now taking the first tentative steps toward change and to encourage those congregations that have been at it awhile and are growing weary along the way.

Several factors have positioned me to observe the spiritual habits of transforming congregations. I have lived most of my life in the western United States, the part of America sociologists recognize has long embodied the post-Christendom culture other parts of the country are only now anticipating. In some western communities, less than three percent of the population worships in a church or synagogue during the week.[1] Many people mark "none" when asked to identify their religious affiliation. Having spent my entire ministry in this "none zone," I have never known anything other than the church on the margins.

Now I live in Montana where isolated communities are known for their rugged and fierce individualism. Montanans mind their own business and keep their own counsel. Strong family ties and established friendships among long-time residents make it hard for newcomers to find community. On the weekends, as in other parts of the nation, recreational sports compete with church for people's time and attention.

I am an ordained minister in the Christian Church (Disciples of Christ), a small denomination that began as a movement for Christian unity on the American frontier in the early 1800s. It now refers to itself as a "Movement for Wholeness." Frequently called simply "The Disciples," we center our lives in Jesus Christ but we do not use any written creed as a test of right belief. We value freedom and diversity of opinion. Like other historic Protestant denominations, we expect each person to read the Bible and to seek to understand the meanings of Biblical passages in light of the historical context in which they were written. Each congregation takes responsibility for its own life and ministry and binds itself to live in unity with the whole church. Lay people lead alongside pastors, and women and men serve together in all the roles of church organization. Whenever The Disciples worship, we come around a common table, sharing the bread and cup of communion in celebration of God's abundant generosity.

I am the spouse of a congregational pastor who struggles to find his way in the changing landscape of ministerial leadership. Sometimes frustrated because many of the skills he honed during thirty years of ministry no longer seem needed, he is seeking to learn new ways of pastoring and leading a spiritual community committed to inclusivity and mission. Often surprised by the new kind of church emerging, his hope is enlivened when he sees individuals, relationships, and structures transformed by the touch of the gospel.

I am a Regional Minister and a Church Consultant. Those ministries have given me the opportunity to walk alongside leaders of many different denominations in hundreds of churches over the last twenty-five years. I have seen congregations at all points of their life cycle and have studied congregational dynamics first hand. I have worked with faith communities of various sizes in cities, in towns, and on prairies that are struggling and straining to see the new thing God is doing among and through them. I have coached pastors during times of stability, change, conflict, and harmony.

From this vantage point, I have noticed that the congregations which find their way to vitality hold in common the practice of twelve spiritual habits. (A list of them also appears in Appendix A.)

1. Transforming congregations root themselves in the power and presence of God through prayer.
2. Transforming congregations listen to the voice of the Spirit which speaks through sign, symbol, and metaphor.
3. Transforming congregations continue to grow spiritually.
4. Transforming congregations align their purpose with God's purpose of peace, security, and justice for all.

5. Transforming congregations engage in ministry where there is suffering.

6. Transforming congregations frequently testify to the activity of the Spirit that works in and through their vision, mission, and core values.

7. Transforming congregations become inclusive communities by welcoming the stranger and forming mutual relationships.

8. Transforming congregations question religious perspectives that have lost credibility and engage in robust theological dialogue about issues posed by change.

9. Transforming congregations build capacity and expect accountability.

10. Transforming congregations cultivate gratitude which helps them see God's provision of plenty in their midst.

11. Transforming congregations collaborate with other partners in order to serve God's intentions in the place where they live.

12. Transforming congregations choose to take strategic actions that heal personal, social, and environmental injuries.

The transforming congregations described in this book are real; they all identify with one of the historic Protestant traditions named above. Other books and articles already have told in depth the stories of congregations like them who have been traveling the transformation road, learning to serve in new ways in the places where they are located. This book describes the pattern those churches make when seen together which reveals the spiritual habits they hold in common. Those spiritual habits serve as lights on lampstands, marking the way for other congregations trying to navigate new paths in the 21st Century.

It is not possible to see all the changes the future will require of historic Protestant congregations; but churches today do not need to see that far ahead, they only need to navigate from signpost to signpost, to be courageous, faithful and open, trusting that the Spirit will guide them the whole way.

TABLE OF CONTENTS

INTRODUCTION
BECOMING NEW

The important thing is this:
to be able at any moment to sacrifice what we are
for what we may become.[2]
– Charles Du Bos

Transforming congregations adapt to changing conditions. As situations arise in their neighborhoods, they respond nimbly, sacrificing what they are in order to become new. One of the best examples of a transforming congregation adapting to its environment comes from the country of El Salvador. It is the story of the church of Fe y Esperanza (Faith and Hope). Congregations in the United States can learn from the ways it took creative action when circumstances called for new ministries.

The year was 1982 and El Salvador was embroiled in a civil war. Death squads invaded villages. They kidnapped children to train as soldiers and burned food supplies and homes. Over 70,000 villagers were murdered. Others fled for their lives. Six hundred of those men and women who escaped found their way to a piece of property in the countryside purchased by the Evangelical Lutheran Church in America at the request of the Lutheran Church in El Salvador. That land served as a sanctuary for those escaping the ravages of war.

It was there that Fe y Esperanza began. Volunteers from other historic Protestant churches helped out wherever they could while the Green Cross tended to wounds. Families cooked food in shared outdoor kitchens as was their custom back home in their own villages. Together they lived in long cinder block buildings that provided the bare minimum shelter. When soldiers came, church leaders hid the refugees in underground bunkers. For seven years, the mission of Fe y Esperanza was to provide a safe haven for those who had been displaced.

But in 1987, things changed. A peace accord was signed. Some villagers went back to the places where they had grown up, hoping to reconnect with members of their families. Others began constructing settlements right around Fe y Esperanza. Now, because the needs of the people had changed, Fe y Esperanza became something different. The leaders built a large hall and classrooms on the property and began offering worship services, Sunday school, youth groups, and seminars about how to prevent violence. They set up workshops where people created traditional Salvadoran art to support themselves. Once Fe y Esperanza had offered safe space for refugees; but its new mission became helping people build for the future.

Now, Fe y Esperanza has altered its mission focus again. It teaches resettled families ways to sustain themselves on small parcels of land through the latest techniques in organic agriculture. Families can produce the food they need right where they live using methods that care for creation.

In each phase of its ministry, Fe y Esperanza engaged in a specific mission determined by its context. It adapted itself to the changing circumstances of its neighbors. It listened to the people it was called to serve in order to discern their most critical needs. It strategized about how to meet those needs and took action. Then when the need for a particular ministry was over, Fe y Esperanza stopped whatever it had been doing in order take up a new, more necessary ministry. Over and over again, the church willingly died in order to be reborn as a more effective instrument of God's love. It became new in order to be relevant.

CHANGING CONDITIONS

Even though most historic Protestant congregations in the United States do not serve in a war zone, the circumstances in which the church is called to minister keep changing. Here are some conditions which characterize the present:

1. GLOBALIZATION reduces both geographic distance and time. Now, it is possible to buy a Coke in both Kansas City and New Delhi, to shop at The Gap in both Seattle and Shanghai. A computer made in Indonesia may be shipped to a British customer and serviced by a technician in India. When revolutions take place in the Middle East, news sources all over the world simultaneously receive reports and photographs from individuals communicating via satellite.

2. INTERDEPENDENCE creates a web of relationships so every individual action affects the whole. Bank failure in the United States distresses the domestic housing and job markets while affecting the banks in Europe as well. The world now is so interconnected that a small incident can set off a chain of events with far reaching consequences. An economic or political crisis in one nation affects other nations. An ecological disaster in one location holds implications for the entire planet.

3. DISPERSED POWER results from readily accessible information that comes from many sources. People do not depend on experts to give them the answers. They do not endow the clergy, the Bible, or the church with assumed moral authority. They chat, blog, post, and click to express their own views within a marketplace of ideas and opinions.

4. RACIAL AND RELIGIOUS DIVERSITY increases as waves of refugees and immigrants change the cultural, political, and economic backdrop in many North American communities. On the street, residents hear others speaking languages they cannot understand and they associate with neighbors who have a variety of skin tones, religious beliefs, values, customs, and viewpoints.

5. EVOLVING COMPLEXITY characterizes the post-modern world where species continue to evolve and systems continue to interact with each other. The theory of cause and effect has given way to new explanations that consider random actions and reactions. Where once leaders relied on linear step-by-step problem-solving to provide answers, now they recognize rational thought as only one way of knowing.[3]

6. NEW ETHICAL QUESTIONS present themselves as science and technology continue to make new discoveries and to invent new tools. Who should have access to innovations? How should such innovations be used? What affect do new advances have on life and death issues? Current generations face alternatives that their grandparents never imagined.

7. A GROWING GAP BETWEEN RICH AND POOR exists in the United Sates where a tiny one percent of the population owns forty percent of the wealth.[4] In the global community North Americans devour eighty-five percent of the world's goods and services even though they make up only one-fifth of the world's population.[5]

8. THE END OF NON-RENEWABLE PLANETARY RESOURCES such as drinking water and fossil fuel is now a reality. Deserts encroach, seas rise, and storms grow larger and more destructive as the climate changes. Violence erupts over who will control the diminishing food supply. Some parts of earth are becoming more crowded.

Meanwhile, rather than responding to these cultural shifts, most historic Protestant congregations today continue to hold onto an anachronistic way of life from a bygone era that renders the church irrelevant. Sociologist Nancy Ammerman calls that way of life "Golden Rule" Christianity.[6]

GOLDEN RULE CHRISTIANITY

The majority of Golden Rule Christians are Anglo-North Americans who build their lives around the principle of treating others as they would like to be treated. They do not go overboard about their religion. They see religion as only one aspect of life, as a personal set of beliefs that individuals freely choose and do not discuss outside the church building. Golden Rule Christians feel no need to impose their beliefs on others, neither do they find it necessary to change the whole world; rather, they are content to do good within their own circle of family and friends.

Golden Rule Christianity was forged when the GIs came home from fighting in Germany and Japan. Those returning veterans and their families voluntarily joined the church much like they joined other organizations. At church they could build relationships, make business contacts, and create friendships that filled the void of relatives who lived far away. New parents found a wholesome, intergenerational place to raise their children at church where they focused on the power of positive thinking[7] after the gruesome carnage of war.

Back then, the culture and the church supported each other, blurring the distinctions between the civic and the religious. The name of God was invoked both in Girl Scout meetings and in Bible studies. The American flag graced both the room where the Rotary Club met and the church sanctuary. On Sunday morning, businesses closed because it was assumed that most people would be in worship.

People in the Golden Rule Church did not spend much time defining Christianity. They did not have to. The church's habits of helpfulness, civilized behavior, niceness, and friendliness were values they held in common with the conventional Anglo-American culture.

The Golden Rule Church was a destination. People "went to" church. Time spent in church was the measure of faithfulness. Successful congregations were the ones that could afford a big building, that increased their budget each year, and that added more and more programs to serve a growing number of members who joined.

In the Golden Rule Church, it was the job of the pastor to lead the flock. The minister was expected to preach, to teach, to administer the sacraments, and to single-handedly care for church members. One of the main ministerial tasks was visiting. The pastor was to call on church members both in the hospital and in their homes, focusing attention on the sick, the bereaved, and those who could no longer get out of the house to go to church. The rest of the minister's week was taken up with preparing engaging Bible studies and planning an inspiring sermon.

For Golden Rule Christians, worship was the centerpiece of church life. Each Sunday, the order of the service was pretty much the same. The tone was quiet reverence and those who were up front moved with dignity, formality, and orchestrated precision. The worshiping body was usually fairly homogeneous with regard to class, race, and ethnicity.

The Golden Rule Church provided a social life as well as a religious life for its members. Classes, recreational sports leagues, and fellowship events filled the church calendar. Each week, a small army of volunteers kept those programs running by serving meals, teaching classes, leading youth groups and repairing the church building.

I grew up in the Golden Rule Church. My parents counted on the congregation where they were members to socialize me into middle-class American culture and to teach me to value moral character, good citizenship and polite behavior. In the Golden Rule Church, Bible verses and simplistic aphorisms were used to convey in short, pithy bits of wisdom the essence of the Christian life. "Be ye kind one to another" (Ephesians 4:32) was emblazoned across the wall of my Sunday School classroom, probably in hopes that it would inspire discipline. Almost every week, I heard the person giving the Call to Offering in worship remind us, "God loves a cheerful giver" (2 Corinthians 9:7). When a disheveled man smelling of alcohol showed up on the front steps of the church asking for a handout, adults often would cluck their tongues and invoke the quote they thought came from the Bible: "God helps those who help themselves."

The Golden Rule Church made sense of the world by ignoring much of its complexity, viewing reality from a frame of reference that relied on dualistic categories of right and wrong, good and bad, insiders and outsiders. Although the insiders might help the outsiders with good works, it was important to maintain the social boundary between the two groups. Insiders were the ones who gave money and received services provided by the church when they were sick and when their families went through passages such as births, coming of age, marriage, and death. Outsiders were the object of the church's charity.

We live in a time when religion in general and Golden Rule Christianity in particular have lost credibility with the public. People today do not look for an organization to join. They do not seek to add church activities into a schedule that is already too full. They do not want more things to do. They do not find much in positive thinking, polite behavior, simplistic aphorisms, or dualistic thinking that allows them to navigate the complexity of a global culture. They are not interested in acquiring a set of beliefs that assure them a place in heaven. They do not see the church as the authority with a monopoly on the truth. They do not find meaning in orchestrated formality. They do not have to come to church in order to connect with friends.

Adherence to religion in the United States is declining. Thirty years ago, thirty-eight percent of North Americans attended at least one religious service each week; today only twenty-five percent do.[8] In 1970, thirty percent of the population worshiped occasionally; today only sixteen percent attends church or synagogue every so often.[9] Although the decline of the church can be attributed, in part, to a decrease in the birthrate and population shifts from farm to city and from north to south, many of those who are no longer affiliated with a church say they left because Golden Rule Christianity became irrelevant.[10]

RESPONDING TO CULTURAL SHIFTS

How does the Golden Rule Church respond to such critique? Some congregations continue to carry on as if they are still living in the 1950s. They do not believe it is the task of the church to be relevant in changing times. They see the church as a refuge, a stable tradition amid the shifting sands of the world outside its doors. They stick to the old prayer book, the old hymnal, and the old rituals that provided comfort and constancy in the past, claiming the church must stand firm in the eternal truths it proclaims rather than allowing ephemeral cultural trends to shape its ministry.

Some try to take shelter from the changes taking place on the cultural landscape. They welcome only those visitors who look like them, who fit into the unspoken norms of church life, and who have the potential to replace the members they are losing. They try to protect themselves from the dangers of pluralism, diversity, and uncertainty. They build large worship centers that create an isolated environment. They listen only to Christian music, Christian radio, and Christian television. Some ultra-large congregations actually resemble theme parks where people can find one homogeneous brand of education, entertainment, literature, and social life, all without leaving the compound.

Some Golden Rule congregations actively work to reverse the changes that have occurred in the culture. They feel disenfranchised and angry about the church losing the power, prestige, and privilege by which it benefited in years gone by. Hoping to return to the way things used to be, they seek to reclaim the authority of the clergy, the certainty of scripture, and the social order of the past in which various segments of society accepted their assigned roles and stayed in their places.

Some admit they do not know how to respond in any meaningful way to the changes taking place in the culture around them. They do not understand why the creativity and joy that used to permeate the church's life and work walked out the door. They do not know why their children and grandchildren choose to spend Sunday mornings sleeping in, reading the morning newspaper, drinking coffee, going to the lake or the ski slope, attending soccer games, shopping, or doing projects around the home instead of choosing to come to worship. So, they try harder, doing the same things they have always done with the wishful hope they will achieve different results.

Some try to make superficial changes in order to attract new members. They trade their pews for chairs, add espresso bars and information booths, and offer mid-week classes that range from aerobics to parenting skills to money management.

They install screens and projectors in their worship space, add drums and bass guitars to the keyboard that accompanies congregational singing, do away with worship bulletins in favor of PowerPoint slides more familiar to "seekers," and proclaim an upbeat message packaged in the familiar and comfortable style of the pop-culture. They focus on offering an excellent religious product for the clientele that comes through the doors of the church.

Some Golden Rule congregations can see that the church needs to change but they do not have the will to lead the congregation to do the hard work necessary to adapt to the world of the 21st Century. Recognizing that doing nothing will result in the congregation's demise, they focus on making sure there is enough money in the bank to keep the church's doors open just long enough to host the funerals for its existing members. They do not have the energy to take another path.

Yet some congregations can see that Golden Rule Christianity has become obsolete. They relinquish it, even without knowing what will take its place by admitting that its view of reality, its values, and its strategy for living are no longer relevant in today's world. It takes great courage to take such a step. At first, some churches feel disoriented as they realized that the familiar ground where they once stood has crumbled away. Some wonder if they will ever have a new place to stand. Others feel exhilarated by new learning; but over time, they too may experience anxiety, dismay, and even panic as they continue to navigate uncharted waters. Yet transforming congregations resist the temptation to clutch more tightly to what has been, to try harder, to exert more control or, conversely, to give up, to lose hope. Instead, they surrender themselves over and over to a future they cannot see; they step out into a unknown future, trusting the Sacred Spirit to show them the way.

They become students of the Christian faith, going back to its source: rediscovering who Jesus was, the wisdom he taught, and the way of life he called people to live. They become students of the changing landscape of the 21st Century: learning how technology has altered the perception of time, space, and authority. They become students of their communities: listening to the needs of their neighbors. They acknowledge that new realities create new questions that can only be addressed by a wide number of people working together:

- How can we live as citizens of an inter-connected global society with people who are not like us?
- How can we make wise and ethical choices in a world with an increasing number of options?
- How can we address multi-faceted problems which have no simple solutions?
- Transforming congregations allow themselves to be changed by the power of the Spirit into new creations capable of telling an old story in a way that is relevant to a new time.

Those transforming congregations do not focus on the church's survival; they look outward to the needs of the community around the church. They do not try to escape into simple certainty that ignores the complexity of the 21st Century world. Like Fe y Esperanza, they engage in mission with their neighbors. They connect with the power and the presence of the Spirit in order to see in new ways. They connect with a purpose that is larger than their own self-interest, aligning their will with God's vision of the new creation. They create a safe place where a diversity of people can learn and grow together. They connect with earth and with the global community in all its complexity and messiness in order to make a practical difference in the life of the planet.

QUESTIONS FOR REFLECTION

1. How do the conditions which characterize the present affect those living today?

2. Where have you seen evidence of those conditions in your own community?

3. Can you describe a time when your congregation adapted how they were doing things in order to meet a new need? What happened?

4. What might the Spirit be calling your congregation to do now in order to become a new creation that is relevant and responsive to your neighbors' needs?

Connecting with the Spirit Within

SPIRITUAL HABIT 1
PRAYING

The exquisite risk is twofold:
the risk to still our own house so that Spirit can come through
so that we might drop into the vital nature of things,
and the risk to then let that beautiful knowing
inform our days.[11]

— Mark Nepo

"The greatest change took place in our congregation when we started praying." The man had been asked to share at a gathering about his church's journey as a transforming congregation. "Oh, we've always said prayers as a church; but now we're really praying. Our leaders gather once a week to pray for our ministry, to pray for people in the congregation, and to pray for each other. It's helped us connect with each other and with God in new ways."

"We all felt a little awkward at first," another woman from the same congregation said. She turned to another woman sitting next to her in the circle. "I guess that sounds awful, doesn't it? That praying was so awkward for church people? But it was. Then our pastor taught us several different ways we could pray at home. Last Lent, we each committed to thirty minutes of prayer every day. I couldn't imagine what I would find to pray about for that amount of time, but I gave it a try. Sometimes I journaled. Sometimes I read something inspiring, or listened to music, or prayed while I walked, or just meditated in silence. The time was up before I knew it!"

"Learning to pray sure was the first step for our congregation." A leader from another church spoke up. "I don't think we could have taken all the other steps we've taken as a congregation if we hadn't begun with prayer. Now the church feels … I guess I would say less religious and more spiritual."

Another woman from the other side of the circle joined in. "I would say we're calmer too. The little things don't stir us up like they used to. It all started for our congregation when we installed a labyrinth in our church hall. People from the neighborhood started coming in to walk it during their lunch hour and we've used it for several prayer services."

"On Wednesday nights, we have a worship service that's just quiet music playing for a half hour. I come because it's a place of rest and it makes a difference in the rest of my week," a younger woman added. "Our church feels more peaceful than it did a few years ago. Even our business meetings seem to have a different tone. We've shifted from an organization which talks about God to a community which connects with God."

Transforming congregations learn to rely, not on their own power, but on the power of the Spirit that runs like sap through the core of their being. Like a tree planted by water, those who pray send out roots by the stream of God's life-giving love.

> *It shall not fear when heat comes,*
> *and its leaves shall stay green;*
> *In the year of drought it is not anxious,*
> *and it does not cease to bear fruit.*   (Jeremiah 17:7-8)

Prayer provides transforming congregations with the resilience they need to thrive even in stressful times.

COPING WITH ANXIETY

Change in the cultural landscape creates anxiety for North Americans. Grief due to a loss of status, members, and support causes anxiety in the church. Anxiety is the automatic reaction to a threat, real or imagined.[12] Anxiety in the human body makes muscles tighten and jaws clench. It creates the feeling of being bound up and weighed down. Anxiety in the Body of Christ causes narrow-minded thinking, irritability, and hopelessness. Over time, it can become disorienting and debilitating.

In order to cope with anxiety, people living today often fall back on two coping strategies their cave-dwelling ancestors used when their stress level was raised by the threat of a large beast: fight or flight. When people are anxious, they may work harder, believing that success is all up to their own efforts, or they may give up, believing that they can do nothing to change the situation. On the one hand, they try to ease anxiety by controlling it; on the other, they try to flee anxiety by escaping it.[13]

Some people fight anxiety by trying to micro-manage those people, places, or things over which they believe they still have influence. They construct a sense of order amid chaos by reducing growing complexity into simplistic categories. To keep intact those categories, however, requires disregarding the growing diversity in the world by limiting their relationships to include only those who are like them. Eventually, they may begin making a habit of avoiding contact with people, events, or ideas that challenge their way of thinking and ignoring conflicting information by mentally categorizing it as unimportant.[14]

Control can also take the form of blame. Rather than engage in thoughtful reflection that leads to responsible action when anxiety appears, people divide themselves into political camps of like-minded people and alienate those who do not share their same beliefs. They view only the network that gives them the news with the slant that matches their own ideology. They read only read the books and visit only the websites that confirm beliefs they already hold. They look for scapegoats to impute—all for the sake of maintaining the illusion that they are in charge of what is happening.

Escape is the second way people try to ease anxiety. They flee to the private realm in order to isolate themselves from the distress of the public arena. Ironically, they insulate themselves from the unpleasantness of the changing world by becoming consumers of its products. They invest in a large number of diversions the technological industry makes available to them. Those who can afford to, come home to large houses surrounded by acreage in gated communities and hole up in front of big screen televisions in home theaters where movies and shows provide respite from the complications of daily life. They engross themselves in worlds created by video games. They lose themselves in applications available on their mobile phones. They immerse themselves in the traumas of celebrities or in the battles of their favorite sports teams, living vicariously through the triumphs and defeats of the stars.

Congregations often try to escape the discomfort of anxiety by attempting to make everyone in the church feel comfortable. To do so, they circulate surveys and then build their ministry around the personal preferences of the majority of their members, or make compromises to make the most people happy. They design worship with something for everyone and chase after those who leave the church, assuring them that the congregation will construct its ministry around their specific desires.

Congregations that try to appease everyone may feel harmonious, but their interactions often stay at a surface level. In order to avoid conflict, they often remain passive and avoid making decisions by continually dithering. In order to avoid taking responsibility, they often invest in an outside source of authority that will make decisions for them. They look to the expert who will provide a quick fix, or to the pastor who will save the church.

Other congregations escape anxiety by pretending everything is fine. They hunker down and ignore the changes that have taken place around them. Their participants busy themselves with their individual lives, their individual careers, their individual families and friends. They go to church to have their needs met by the minister who has been hired or appointed to do just that. As long as the clergyperson is doing the job, he or she is allowed to stay. If the pastor begins making them uncomfortable by calling the church to be something more, it is likely that pastor will be fired or reassigned.

Control and escape may provide respite from anxiety in the short-run, but as coping strategies, they do not make for healthy communities in the long-run. Over-functioning by taking responsibility for everything leads to exhaustion; under-functioning by bolting the door against distress leads to loneliness. Keeping harmony leads to superficiality; cutting oneself off from others leads to fragmentation. No matter how much power North Americans gain, how much they buy, how much happiness they pursue, they are left with the nagging truth that they cannot control everything nor can they escape every discomfort that life dishes out.

Prayer calls transforming congregations to solitude rather than escape, to letting-go rather than control. Through prayer, they find serenity, even amid the noise and chaos of change. Prayer connects them to the power and presence of the Spirit that resides within and among them.

CONNECTING TO THE SACRED SPIRIT

Because the Spirit is an invisible life-force, the Bible uses the language of poetry to describe its nature and activity. It depicts the Spirit as a bird that descends from out of the blue,[15] as a fire that comes to rest upon individuals, giving them the ability to speak the words of God,[16] and as power that fills people up so that the selfish ego disappears.[17] It portrays the Spirit as life-giving water that pours out over a thirsty land, like a stream that brings nourishment and growth to dry ground.[18] It describes the Spirit as a lover that captivates,[19] causing people to lose track of time and overwhelming them with wonder, adoration, and gratitude. It affirms that it is possible to dwell in the Spirit[20] and that the Spirit can lift people up out of the mundane like a whirlwind carrying individuals through mystical visions into another reality.[21]

The Christian tradition teaches Jesus was so filled up with the Spirit that he became a Spirit-Man, both fully divine and fully human. John's Gospel claims what was possible for Christ is also possible for Christ's followers: "To all received him, who believed in this name, he gave power to become children of God" (John 1:12). Just as Jesus became a Spirit-Man, other ordinary people can become spiritual human beings filled with the power of God and enlivened by that creative Spirit. For the Apostle Paul, living "in the Spirit" was the same as living "in Christ."[22] Throughout his letters, he interchangeably used the phrases "Spirit," "Spirit of God," and "Spirit of Christ." He understood the presence of the Risen Christ to be the same as the Spirit of God. When the church dwelt in Christ, it could access the energy of the Spirit and live in the fullness of life.

The Bible described the activity of the Spirit as wind and breath: *ruach* (roo-ach) in Hebrew and *pneuma* (noo-ma) in Greek. The book of Genesis proclaimed that the Sacred Spirit had been present since the creation of the world when it swept over the waters like a wind.[23] That wind-like energy was creative and life-giving but also unpredictable and uncontrollable. "The wind blows where it chooses," Jesus told Nicodemus. "You hear the sound of it but you do not know where it comes from or where it goes" (John 3:8a).

The book of Acts described the wind blowing through Jesus' followers, taking away their fear and empowering them to speak with boldness. On Pentecost, the disciples were all together in one place when, suddenly, they heard a sound like the rush of a violent wind. It filled the whole house where they sat. Then flames of fire appeared among them and one flame rested on each one of them. All of them were filled with the Holy Spirit and began to speak in other languages as the Spirit gave them ability.[24] The Spirit came upon the disciples unannounced and enabled them to communicate in a global context.

Centuries earlier, the prophet Joel had heard God speak of such a time when the power of the Spirit would be made available, not to just a few religious leaders, but to everyone.

> *"I will pour out my Spirit on all flesh," God told Joel.*
> *"Your sons and your daughters shall prophesy,*
> *Your old men shall dream dreams*
> *And your young men shall see visions*
> *Even on the male and female slaves,*
> *In those days, I will pour out my spirit."*   (Joel 2:28b-29)

The Spirit could not be contained in one nation's customs or language; it had been set loose in the world and could be found everywhere, if people only had eyes to see it.

The second Creation Story described the Spirit as the breath of life. God breathed life into the nostrils of the *adam* (human) made from the *adamah* (humus) and that breath animated the dirt causing it to become a self-aware human being who could think, choose, and take action.[25] The Psalmist expressed a common belief of ancient people:

When you take away their breath they die
And return to their dust.
When you send forth your spirit, they are created;
And you renew the face of the ground   (Psalm 104: 29b 30)

For there to be life, the breath of the Spirit had to be present.

The book of Ezekiel told the story of a prophet who had a vision of a valley full of dry bones. God spoke to the bones through Ezekiel, "I will cause breath to enter you and you shall live" (Ezekiel 37:5b). God laid sinews on the bones and caused flesh to come upon them, but muscles and skin alone did not make for life. It was only when the breath entered the bodies that they lived.[26] The breath – the *ruach* – was the life-force, the energy that caused them to become living human beings who could stand on their own two feet.[27]

In the Gospel of John we read that the disciples were holed up in a locked room after Jesus' crucifixion because they were anxious. But Jesus came and stood among them and said, "Peace be with you." He breathed on them and said to them, "Receive the Holy Spirit." Then he sent them out to continue the work God sent him to do.[28] The breath enlivened them and allowed them to carry on Jesus' ministry in the world.

THE SPIRITUAL HABIT OF PRAYER

In transforming congregations a high percentage of individuals take time each day to engage in the ancient Christian practice of listening prayer. Listening prayer connects them with the empowering and enlivening Spirit. In Mark Nepo's words, it allows them to still their own house and drop into the vital nature of things. It expands the eyes of their heart so that they can see the underlying oneness of all creation. It allows them to align their heart with the heart of God. It bonds them to a Spiritual energy that dispels anxiety and teaches them what it means to live as the authentic Self that is created in the divine image.

"I didn't know how I would fit prayer into my life," one young mother confessed, "but now I get up a half hour before the kids get up. When I take time to pray, it settles me down and gives me a sense of peace. That peace allows me to take on the challenges in the rest of the day without getting rattled by them. Prayer helps me tell the difference between the voice of God and all the other voices in my life. I wouldn't trade my morning time for anything!"

Listening prayer comes in many forms including but not limited to:

1. PRAYING WITH THE IMAGINATION: Ignatius of Loyola encouraged Christians to enter into a Biblical passage and to use their senses to explore the scene. What does it look like? What sounds can you hear? What can you smell? What conversations do you overhear? What happens next? What do you do? What does the Spirit say to you as a result of your immersion in that place?

2. TRANSPOSING PRAYER: Augustine of Hippo taught Christians to transpose the words of a Biblical passage to their lives. For example, if the passage is about the "bent-over woman, the reader reflects on what or who is "bent over"—physically, spiritually, socially—in their world. They listen to Jesus saying to the woman (and to those situations in their own lives) "You are set free from your ailment."[29]

3. *LECTIO DIVINA* (DIVINE READING): The Benedictine Tradition taught people how to read through a Biblical passage slowly, listening to the whole passage. Next, it encouraged them to read through it a second time, listening to the word or phrase that seems to speak directly to their own lives. Finally, it invited them to read it a third time, considering what action the phrase might be guiding them to take.

4. CENTERING PRAYER: A book by a 14th Century anonymous author entitled *The Cloud of Unknowing* taught a form of prayer in which a person sits in silence with eyes closed and focuses on one word or phrase of their choosing that invites the presence of the sacred Spirit.

5. CONTEMPLATIVE PRAYER: Hildegard of Bingen and others taught Christians to focus on a scene or an object from creation, allowing it to reveal to them some aspect of God's nature and purpose. (See Appendix B for a hand-out on the various forms of Listening Prayer.)[30]

However, it is not just individuals who engage in listening prayer in transforming congregations; the whole church corporately prays together in many different ways. Prayer keeps the congregation grounded in the power and presence of God. The church's life together becomes a dialogue with God in which it tries to listen and respond to the leading of the Spirit. Prayer opens it up to wonder and gratitude for the gift of life. It gives the congregation time to be self-reflective, to notice what is going on instead of just plunging headlong through life unaware of the presence of the Holy in its midst.

In transforming congregations, leaders pray together weekly and the congregation prays every time it worships together. Prayers are spoken aloud by the pastor and lay people offer public prayer as well. Often there is a group within a transforming congregation that prays for those in need as its sole mission. Sometimes that group walks the streets and prays for their neighbors. Sometimes it gathers prayer requests and offers intercessory prayer on behalf of those who wrote them. Many transforming congregations also make time during their worship life for corporate silence, for being alone together in the stillness. Some offer entire worship services planned to allow for contemplation, making use of simple, repetitive, quiet songs.

Others practice the Biblical tradition of anointing with oil or placing hands on a person seeking healing and wholeness. Unlike some Pentecostal traditions that may promise a "cure" by such actions, transforming congregations seek only to be a conduit for the Spirit's power, leaving the nature of the healing up to God's good grace.

Making intentional time to connect with the power and presence of the Spirit, both corporately and individually, allows

transforming congregations to practice resting in God without
having to control anything. It teaches them to trust the leading of
the Spirit, even when they do not have all the answers. It allows
them to reframe their understanding of what it means to be human.
When they take time to pray, they learn to see themselves not just
as those who consume, but also as those who create, not just as
those who seek comfort, but also as those who are called and sent
for the sake of the world.

When transforming congregations take time for prayer they
not only reduce the stress in their life, they also subvert the claim
made by the consumer culture that there is not enough time to do
what needs to be done. Prayer allows transforming congregations
to let go of the anxiety that causes them to choose the safe, the
expedient, and comfortable. It helps them to make bold decisions
in order to become the people they believe God is calling them to
be. It allows them to say yes to God's future, even before they know
what that future will bring.

QUESTIONS FOR REFLECTION

1. What causes you to feel anxious? How do you behave when
   you are anxious?
2. Which metaphor for the Spirit from the Bible particularly
   captures your imagination? Why?
3. What distractions keep you from making prayer a priority in
   your life?
4. What could you do to create a set-aside time of prayer amid
   the noise and clamor of each day?

bird
fire
water
power
lover

SPIRITUAL HABIT 2
WAKING UP

Life is no passing memory of what has been nor the remaining pages
in a great book waiting to be read.
It is the opening of eyes long closed.[31]

– David Whyte

The Gospel of Luke tells the story of a couple traveling on foot along the seven-mile path to Emmaus from Jerusalem after Jesus' execution.[32] Along the way, a man came up and started walking alongside the couple, but they did not recognize him. Since he seemed oblivious to the events of the week, the couple recounted all that had happened in Jerusalem. "We had hoped that he was the one who would deliver Israel," they said. Then the man began to tell them how the recent events were a fulfillment of all that the Torah and the prophets had taught.

When they got to the edge of the village, the man acted as if he were going on, but the couple invited him to their home. "Stay and have supper with us," they said. "It's late and the sun is going down." So he went into the house and sat down at the table with them. Taking the bread, he blessed and broke and gave it to them. At that moment, they suddenly woke up and recognized Jesus. Then he vanished from their sight.

"Didn't our hearts burn as he talked with us on the road?" they asked each other. Immediately, they were up and on their way back to Jerusalem. When they arrived, the disciples and their other friends told them, "Simon has seen Jesus!" Then the couple related what had happened on the road and how they had recognized Jesus when he broke the bread.

Educator, clinical psychologist and theologian James Loder calls the events in Emmaus that night a "convictional moment." Convictional moments are times when we wake up to the activity

of the Spirit, when our eyes open to a larger reality that changes
how we choose to act, and when we perceive the whole that is
more than the sum of its parts. According to Loder, convictional
moments follow a pattern with five movements:[33]

1. A RESTLESS INCOHERENCE that comes about when we
    experience something new which stands in opposition to what
    we assumed to be true. In this movement we become aware
    of a tension between our need for internal harmony and the
    sense that something is just not fitting. *The travelers had hoped
    that Jesus was the one who would redeem Israel, but with the
    crucifixion, their hopes were shattered.*

2. AN INTERLUDE FOR SCANNING in which we put the
    conflict into the back of our mind. In this movement we may
    randomly, almost passively explore possible ways to resolve
    the tension we feel. *The travelers opened themselves up to the
    teaching of the one who had joined them. They did not engage
    in debate; in fact the story gives the impression that they listened
    almost passively to what the stranger had to say – although later
    they reported that their hearts were burning as he spoke to them
    on the road.*

3. AN INSIGHT FELT WITH INTUITIVE FORCE in
    which we experience an "ah-ha" and are surprised with a
    larger, wholly new outlook that comes to us from beyond
    ourselves, simplifying and unifying the elements that have
    been in conflict. In this movement, the tension not only is
    constructively resolved, but we become "new creations." *In
    the story, that insight took place when Jesus broke the bread.
    The couples' eyes were opened and they experienced an "ah-ha"
    of "seeing," not the "unrecognized visible Presence" who talked
    with them on the road, but the "recognized invisible Presence"
    in their midst.*[34]

4. A PERIOD OF RELEASE AND REPATTERNING in which
    energy once invested in and bound by the inner conflict is
    made available for creative action in light of the new insight.
    As tension is released, we find a new home, and we experience
    a sense of enlargement, a new quality of openness to self and

world.[35] Life appears fresh, wholeness returns, and we are amazed that the struggle which occupied us resolves itself in a surprising way. In this movement we make a bold move, choosing a risky path. *The couple immediately traveled back to Jerusalem in the dark.*

5. A TIME OF INTERPRETATION AND VERIFICATION In which we tell others what happened. In this movement, we put our new way of viewing the world to a public test as we try to live as a new creation. *When the couple compared notes with the disciples, the cohesiveness in the stories verified their truthfulness.*

Looking back over their life together, most transforming congregations can point to one or more convictional moments when the church was surprised by an awakening in which it received insight from beyond itself and changed because of that new perception. Here are some examples of what it sounds like when transforming congregations talk about the experience:

"We thought we knew where we were headed, and then we all read that book together. It changed everything. Now we are approaching our ministry so much differently."

"We were doing pretty much the same thing week after week; then four gay couples joined our church. They made us re-think everything we stood for."

"After the fire we began worshiping in another congregation's sanctuary. That experience freed us up so much, we're not sure we even want to build again."

"I don't know what happened, but all of a sudden we had six autistic children attending our Christian Education program. Boy, did that change how we taught!"

Convictional moments are those times when the church moves forward by leaps rather than by inches. Looking back on those moments, transforming congregations notice how they were joined to the vitality of God, how their consciousness expanded, causing them to feel like they were participating in a mystery larger than themselves. A convictional moment unites a congregation with the energy of the Sacred Spirit that enlivens, dispels fear, and encourages them to engage in compassionate actions beyond selfish pursuits.

For one church, a convictional moment came in the form of an earthquake. Over the years, the church had engaged in many planning retreats. They had talked about reaching out to their changing neighborhood. They had held workshops about contemporary worship. But the church never actually changed. Each time a new idea came up, the affectionate attachment the congregation had for the building would get in the way.

The neighborhood church council wanted to use the kitchen to prepare a community meal once a week for those who were living on the streets; but the leaders rejected the idea because they did not want outsiders using the facility. The local shelter wanted to use the third floor of the church to house families; but the leaders said no because people in the congregation were concerned about germs in the restrooms. A group proposed the congregation host a day center for senior adults; but stairs up and down at every level made that impossible. Some people in the church suggested they hold a lunchtime Bible study in the parlor for students from the community college right across the street; but there was a rule against food in the parlor so the idea was squelched.

"Finally, we were literally blasted out of the church," one leader told me. "It was like the Spirit knew we were never going to get anywhere as long as we were in that building. When an earthquake shattered windows and damaged bricks, the building was so structurally unsound, we couldn't do anything but find a new place to worship." The church moved up the street where it began sharing worship space with another congregation. Later, the two churches became one merged church. Now, that new congregation engages in many neighborhood ministries.

THE AGE OF THE SPIRIT

Theologian Harvey Cox suggests that we in the 21st Century are living at the dawn of a multi-religious, global awakening he calls the "Age of the Spirit." It is a time when individuals across the world experience a new sense of mystery, wonder, and awe that comes from connecting with the power and the presence of the Spirit, relying on that Spirit for guidance and wisdom, and sharing in its creative work.

Yet many historic Protestant congregations tend to be skeptical of anything to do with the Spirit. Some shy away from the term "spirituality" because they associate it with the Pentecostal congregation down the street. They do not want to raise their hands or speak in tongues or dance in the aisles of the church. Some confuse spirituality with the metaphysical philosophy called "spiritualism" made popular by Edgar Cayce. They do not want to get mixed up in trying to contact the dead through séances. Some view spirituality as a fallacy based in superstition. They are used to relying on rationality as their primary way of knowing and associate spirituality with the New Age snake-oil they see in the self-help section of the book store.

Transforming congregations, on the other hand, overcome their distrust of spirituality and unearth a rich and long tradition of Christian teaching related to the Spirit. They develop an understanding of Spirit by first recognizing that it reveals itself through symbols, signs, and metaphors. That means it is not usually perceived through rational logic but through intuitive knowing. To be spiritual is to see with the eyes of the heart, to experience the energizing power of God through whispers, hints, nudges, and insights. The language of spirituality is the language of dreams, stories, and visions—forms that are rather foreign to the Western bias towards objectivity, fact and proof. Yet transforming congregations develop a familiarity with that sort of metaphorical communication and learn to detect those convictional moments when their "hearts burned" in the presence of the sacred.

Transforming congregations understand that the Sacred Spirit resides within each person, that every human being is created in the image of God,[36] blessed by God, and called to live in harmony with the created order. Recognizing that humans often get lost along the way and do not cultivate that divine seed that is their birthright, transforming congregations hold individuals accountable for life-long learning and growth. They teach people how to ground themselves in the sacred presence of God through prayer, to resist evil through acts of justice, and to allow God's power to work through their lives just as it worked through the life of Jesus of Nazareth.[37]

THE SPIRITUAL HABIT OF WAKING UP

Transforming congregations seeking to live in the Spirit claim far more is going in any moment than can be apprehended by the human senses. They recognize the Spirit is at work in the world, freeing the enslaved, energizing the disconsolate, making bold the timid, and bringing peace to the anxious. Yet that Spirit cannot be seen, tasted, touched, smelled, or heard. It can only be known by noticing the results of its work and sometimes those results can only be recognized in hindsight.

That's why for centuries Christians have prayed the "*Prayer of Examen.*"[38] They start by "examining" a day, a week, a month, or a year, allowing the events of that time period to play like a movie in the mind. Then, they seek to see the underlying work of the Spirit in and through those events. They notice where the Spirit seemed to be particularly present in their inner thoughts and experiences, in relationship, in systems and structures of the world, or in the environment of God's creation.[39] (See Appendix C for a hand-out on the *Prayer of Examen.*)

Next, they seek to discern what the Spirit might be offering by way of wisdom or guidance through those past events. Did images show up more than once? Where were there surprising coincidences that resulted in good? When did a door open or a helping hand show up? Viewing a past event as a sort of waking dream helps the church understand the language of the Spirit which often communicates in metaphor, symbol, or sign. It allows congregations to notice the presence of God and to follow the Spirit's energy that opens the way forward.

My friend Doug noticed how the Spirit had been at work, guiding him during an activity as mundane as exchanging a pair of pants at the store. The pants had been sitting around his house for several days but on this particular day, he picked them up and decided to take care of the errand. While he was at the store, he ran into a friend he hadn't seen for several weeks. The friend was in need of support and counsel and the two of them found a place where they could have coffee and conversation. When Doug returned home his wife asked if his trip to the store had been successful. Doug replied, "Yes. But it was not about the pants." He saw the events of the day not just as a series of coincidences, but as the Spirit's guidance.

When transforming congregations awaken to the presence of the Spirit, they begin to see underlying wholeness, vitality, and goodness present everywhere grounding their lives in the power of that presence. As they learn the language of the Spirit they begin to notice larger patterns, relationships and connections. Instead of seeing coincidence, they see God at work. They begin to trust unscheduled events as a form of spiritual guidance.

Yet one does not need to look far to notice the mind's power to deceive itself. Over the years, many have claimed to read the signs or to experience the leading of the Spirit. They have wrongly predicted the end of the world; they have led people into mass suicides, death, and destruction. How do we know something is truly of the Spirit and not just, as Ebenezer Scrooge says, "an undigested bit of beef, a blot of mustard, a crumb of cheese, a fragment of an underdone potato?"[40]

Christian spiritual teachers have long taught that discerning the presence and guidance of the Spirit does not happen in a vacuum. Waking up is only one part of a spiritual practice shaped by scripture, connected to God through prayer, and tested in the context of a spiritual community. Although the activity of the Spirit can be surprising, it will never go against the nature of God and will always lead toward consolation, goodness, and light. Although the guidance of the Spirit is often revealed by non-linear, non-rational thought, it will never go against the voice of reason—it will always make sense.

Transforming congregations wake up to the presence of Spirit in their midst with a sense of humility, confessing that the holy mystery of the sacred can never be fully known, and admitting that

human perceptions may be dead wrong. Yet they do not shy away
from asking the question, "Where is the Spirit at work in our congregation, in our neighborhood, in the life of the world?" They pay
attention to the times when something unexpected interrupts their
best laid plans and give thanks for convictional moments when
they happen. They notice larger patterns in the stories they keep
hearing from both those who come through the church door and
those who live in the neighborhood. They see connections between
those stories and the scriptures they read in worship.

In the power of the Spirit wind, transforming congregations
often find themselves taking risks they never would have imagined
themselves taking before. Some decide to leave their money-con-
suming building behind in order to meet in a more cost-saving
facility or in public space so they have more resources for outreach.
Some choose to start a new ministry to meet the needs of a changing neighborhood. Some dare to get acquainted with strangers and
to form new partnerships. Transforming congregations make bold
decisions about their life and ministry, even when those decisions
make them vulnerable to rejection or scorn. They are always ready
to follow the Spirit in a new direction they had not imagined before.

QUESTIONS FOR REFLECTION

1. Looking back over your life or the life of your congregation,
    what is one time you experienced the "ah-ha" of a convictional
    moment? What happened?

2. Why is an open heart an essential prerequisite to noticing the
    presence and guidance of the Spirit? *Can't do the same old
    things and expect a different outcome.*

3. What might your congregation do to get more comfortable
    with the language of the Spirit? *Read & study the Bible —
    compare then to now — pray*

4. How can your congregation counter some of the dangers that
    engaging in Spiritual discernment might pose? *Leads toward consolation, goodness & light —
    never goes against reason — always makes sense.*

*Many (most) people go through life on auto-pilot —
must learn to really think.*

Act — not re-act!

SPIRITUAL HABIT 3
GROWING

Now I become myself. [41]

— May Sarton

One summer, I registered for the Adult Beach Trail Hike sponsored by my church. I put the required list of items in my pack, laced up my boots and joined the group that had signed up for the experience. We hiked out to Sand Point on the wilderness coast of Washington, set up our tents, and fixed dinner over our backpack stoves. Then we sat around a campfire as we ate.

The next morning after breakfast, the director gathered us together on the beach. "I invite those who want to learn courage today to climb to the top of that headland. Those who would like to cultivate patience, wait for the tide to go out before you hike up to the river. Those who would like to experience beauty, walk south to the tide pools. Those who need some time to reflect, climb up to the top of that rock and sit for a while. Be back here by five o'clock and after dinner we'll share our experiences. Have fun."

Back around the campfire that evening, we all had opportunity to talk about what happened during the day. I was amazed by the depth of the conversation.

"I learned that I can be alone and it's all right," one woman told us. After twenty years of marriage, she and her husband had just divorced.

"I watched the sea anemones open up to be fed," another man said. "Maybe it's time for me to trust that my daily bread's going to be there for me too." He had been out of work for almost a month.

Rather than teaching us what to believe about God, the director simply had provided opportunities for us to connect with God and to be accountable to each other for what we had learned from the experience. We were free to turn in any direction, to make the choice we most needed to make and to listen to the Sacred Spirit. Over the course of the day, we had come to know ourselves more fully. We had discovered spiritual wisdom in commonplace activities. We had found metaphors of nature could become conduits of God's guidance. As we listened to each other's stories that evening, we became community. The experience was transformative.

THE DEVELOPMENTAL JOURNEY

As babies, we quickly come to understand whether or not the environment around us is a safe place where we can receive nurture. As we grow, we watch how authority figures act and we begin to construct frameworks of meaning about the way things are, the way things are supposed to be, and what others expect of us. We learn to please those who have the power to offer us reward or punishment, pleasure or pain.

As we grow, we modify those frameworks of meaning, discovering new lenses through which we can interpret our experience. If our physical maturation is normal, our brains develop the ability to think, not just in literal, concrete terms, but in symbolic, abstract concepts. We also acquire the capacity to evaluate the truth and relevance of the messages we receive.[42] As we develop socially, we learn who we are in relation to our family, other authority figures, our friends, our community, and our world. Eventually we learn to live out of our own integrity rather than conforming to others' expectations.[43] If our moral maturation is normal, we outgrow our childish self-centeredness and gain the ability, not to choose what will give us pleasure in the moment, but to make decisions based on love, justice and what is best for the common good.[44] If our spiritual maturation is normal, we move from learning about God to relating to God and we begin to recognize the holy mystery who lives within us and in whom we live.[45]

As small children, we have little sense of "Self" as a separate being responsible for our own actions. Our family is the extent of our world and we act impulsively to get what we want. We view the world through the lens of magical thinking. We believe our fate is in the hands of powers beyond ourselves. However, we also believe that our fate can be changed by adhering to certain superstitious observances such as not stepping on cracks to keep our mothers' backs intact or being good in order to receive God's blessings and to keep God from punishing us.

In the school-age years, we learn to separate what is real from what is pretend and to curb our impulses in order to please important adults in our lives. We expand our social circle to include a few friends who are like us and other adults who hold positions of power. In order to gain the approval of those authority figures, we learn to follow their rules. As we listen to them define who they think we are, we come to know whether or not we are a human being of worth who can belong and contribute. At this stage, we understand the Bible literally and tend to see God as a rule-giver.

As teens, we usually attach ourselves to a tribe of peers with whom we can identify and we learn to conform to the consensus of that group. Those like-minded friends become the new authority in our life, exerting peer pressure on us. As adolescents, we often try to dress like them, to act like them, and to do what it takes to attain their approval. At this tribal stage, we tend to see God as a personal friend who sides with our group over other groups. Right and wrong become polarized opposites with no in-between.

Yet to develop into healthy adults, we must eventually begin to ask, "What is true about what I have been told?" That question launches us on another phase of the journey of growth and development that lasts the rest of our lives. Instead of adopting others' definitions of who we are, we begin to uncover our true Selves. Instead of seeking the approval of outside authorities, we learn to trust the inner authority of the Spirit. Along the way, as we sort and sift the chaff from the true wisdom we have been given, we begin taking responsibility for our own decisions, separating ourselves from those beliefs and attitudes that do not bring us life.

Because it takes a lot of courage to break ties of loyalty with the tribe of family and friends and to develop our own points of view and systems of belief, our first attempts at self-definition can be awkward and strident. Initially, we exert our independence by rebelling against those who have raised us, sometimes pointing to their hypocrisy while pledging our allegiance to a more idealistic way of life. As we get in touch with who we are, we may declare loudly what we believe and what we don't believe, just so we can hear it spoken aloud and decide if what we are saying really is true.

During young adulthood, we may actually develop an excessive confidence in our own abilities as we choose, for the first time, who and what will receive our allegiance. At first, we may over-identify with a certain thinker or ideology as we wrestle with how we will use our gifts, which relationships will be primary for us, how we will support ourselves, and how we will spend our life energy. We may attach ourselves to teachers or organizations that hold our same values, sometimes using their words to express ourselves before we actually find our own voice.

As young adults, we begin to see God as one who calls us to act as responsible citizens, caring not only for ourselves, but for our neighbors. Rather than imagining God as a man with a beard and a white robe who lives in the sky, we begin to see God in more abstract terms: God is spirit; God is love; God is truth. In young adulthood, we begin to claim our role as servants of such a God, and we begin to develop a "live and let live" attitude about other world religions.

As we enter adulthood, we become aware of a wider world. As we move to another community, attend college, or travel to foreign cultures, we gain other perspectives through which we can now critique our own experience. As we build relationships with those who are not like us, we learn to tolerate and even to appreciate difference. As we personally encounter the needs of others, we develop the capacity for empathy that can propel us toward taking creative and compassionate action in the world.

By the time we reach the middle years of adulthood, our hearts likely have been broken multiple times by death, failure, separation, tragedy, and the loss of valued relationships. We experience dissonance between our realized dreams and the ideals that we once held. We recognize how we have internalized the expectations of others in spite of our best efforts to think and act out of our own individual freedom. We begin to see that the frameworks of meaning we have created for ourselves are too small or too simplistic to contain the complexity of our understanding.

In this mid-life stage of adulthood, we begin to move from independence to interdependence, often realizing that we are part of many different systems, some that hold seemingly conflicting values. As we grow and mature in this stage of life, we start examining deeper, more holistic ways of knowing that allow us to see those conflicting values as paradox. Over time, we may develop the capacity for self-surrender and intimacy without compromising our own integrity as we continue the search for both love and justice.

Some of us in old age discover yet a deeper wisdom that allows us to integrate symbols with pragmatic reality and to consider the fabric of life as a whole. In this last stage of growth, while we still cherish our own individuality, we also make peace with our own failings and losses. We develop a deep appreciation for traditional rites and wisdom, re-appropriating traditional symbols with new meaning. We develop the capacity to see unity beyond paradox as we begin to integrate all the aspects of our being into one cohesive whole.

As we mature as adults, we come to see God as both transcendent and intimate, both abstract and interpersonal—a mystery that we will never fully comprehend. We grow to appreciate that other world religions may have perspectives that can enhance our own understandings of God. Symbols that we rejected earlier in our lives, we reclaim and re-appropriate with new meanings. The separation between the holy and secular disappears—God can be seen in all things.

ARRESTED DEVELOPMENT

Growing up is a natural process fostered by a safe, trustworthy environment, opportunities to try new things, affirmations from those who matter, a sense of belonging, and the security of behavioral boundaries strong enough to be tested. However, not all are given those essential building blocks. As a result, we sometimes find ourselves living in adult bodies while continuing to practice our childish ways. We physically age but continue to construct meaning with a framework that may be appropriate for a less mature person.

As babies, it is normal for us to cry when we are hungry and to scream when we do not get enough attention. All our actions are self-centered. But as adults, when we continue to throw tantrums in order to get our way, when strong impulses of anger or immediate gratification still rule our emotions, when cravings for pleasure or comfort still control us, we become narcissistic and fearful. Growing into a healthy adult involves being able to set aside our need for instant gratification in order to care for others.

As children, it is normal for us to identify with family values, customs, and ways of understanding the world. We avoid punishment by staying away from family taboos and we gain a sense of belonging by adhering to family expectations. However, when we get caught up as adults in an ideological fervor, a cause, or a cult that substitutes for the family loyalty we had as children, that allegiance can hinder our spiritual growth.

As children, we have the capacity for only literal thinking, but when we continue using only that tool to interpret information as adults, we lose out on the rich wisdom and the beautiful poetry that comes through abstraction, imagery, and metaphor. If we continue believing as adults in the superstition and magical thinking of childhood, we can forever get caught in self-defeating acts of blaming, justifying ourselves, or playing the victim and never learn to take responsibility for our own behavior.

When we become teens it is normal for peers to become our authority. We make decisions in order to get others to like us and we take actions calculated to please our friends. But when we continue to seek the external approval of others, we can lose our sense of Self, giving away our power by depending on outside opinions to guide our lives. Over time, we can become stilted, controlling, or consumed with perfectionism. Growing into a healthy adult involves developing a strong self-respect that allows us to know our own heart, to find our own voice, and to be able to stand up to the pressure of our peers.

"When I was a child, I spoke like a child, I thought like a child, I reasoned like a child," the Apostle Paul told the church in Corinth. "When I became an adult, I put an end to childish ways."[46] In order to grow up, we must leave behind immature ways of seeing, knowing, and acting, and travel towards a larger generosity, a deeper trust, and a more complete wisdom. The journey is often painful and includes grief, confusion, and even despair. Yet we also discover joy, peace, gratitude, and creativity as we continue along the path.

Although each of us is unique, our path is part of a common human experience of leaving the familiar, venturing to parts unknown and returning home, changed by our experience. Along the way, we learn to see through an ever-widening aperture that alters our perspective and renders obsolete the old ways of ordering the world. But the maturing process is more than just changing our mind about the way the world works; rather, it consists of allowing older versions of the self to actually pass away in order for new, more complete versions of the Self to be born. Jesus said, "Unless a grain of wheat falls into the earth and dies, it remains just a single grain" (John 12:20). To hold onto the old life leads to death; to relinquish it leads to new life: "For those who want to save their life will lose it, and those who lose their life for my sake will find it" (Matthew 16:25).

It requires a great deal of courage and a healthy self-esteem to keep moving on the journey. So much can distract us from holding our feet to the path. It helps to have others around who also are committed to their own spiritual growth and ongoing development. Yet in the church, it is sometimes hard to find companions who are intentionally seeking to mature in faith. Forty-three percent of those who no longer participate in church life say they could not find others in the congregation to make the spiritual journey with them. They left because they spiritually outgrew the church. They may have been church members for a number of years. They may have been part of congregational programs where they learned basic Christian beliefs, acquired the basic tools for Bible study, and developed the habit of personal prayer. They may even have served in the leadership of the church. But eventually they reached a place where they could no longer develop spiritually in the congregation's environment where those around them only wanted to skate along the religious surface.

THE SPIRITUAL HABIT OF GROWING

Transforming congregations retain adult participants and attract newcomers because they cultivate a climate in the church where life-long learning is expected.

When individuals grow up and mature, the whole body of the church stays healthy and strong. The New Testament letter to the Ephesians put it this way:

> *We must no longer be children, tossed to and fro and blown about by every wind of doctrine, by people's trickery, by their craftiness in deceitful scheming. But speaking the truth in love, we must grow up in every way, into him who is the head, into Christ, from whom the whole body, joined and knit together by every ligament with which it is equipped, as each part is working properly, promotes the body's growth in building itself up in love.*   (Ephesians 4:14-16)

In transforming congregations, adults as well as children and youth explore important questions and even express doubts without fear of judgment or criticism. They pursue knowledge from a variety of sources and seek the inner wisdom of the Spirit.

In many transforming congregations, teaching is carried out in an informal way as individuals share with each other about prayer practices particularly meaningful to them, trade poems or quotations, and recommend books, articles, or films. Church participants take time to deeply listen to each other. As they journey with fellow travelers who also are seeking to grow, they learn how to set aside the ego and live out of a more authentic Self that allows them to be precisely who they are before God and one another. They develop the skill of working with the Spirit in the creation of their own lives. They find out how to identify their vocation, their calling. They learn how to listen to their passion and to the urge to use their gifts for the sake of something more than their own self-interest.

Other transforming congregations more formally create learning opportunities through classes or small groups. Those churches become centers of teaching often known for their ability to educate individuals, both inside and outside the church. Some of those classes or small groups make use of what teacher and activist Parker Palmer calls "third things."[47] Third things are resources other than the voice of the facilitator or the voices of the participants—things like poetry, artwork, music, movement, or stories that circumvent the defenses we constructed in order to keep us from speaking and hearing the truth of the soul. Like those metaphors of nature that caused the hikers to think in surprising ways, third things speak truth "on the slant."[48] Their indirect approach can open the mind in unexpected ways.

In larger settings, transforming congregations often use visual media to open minds.[49] They intentionally choose to invite those voices into the educational setting who can offer an alternative to the theological assumptions, world views, or methods of scripture study held by participants. Given ample opportunity for reflection within the context of trustworthy community, many people in transforming congregations report feeling intellectually liberated by new approaches to understanding God, by different perspectives from around the globe, or by scholarly information about how the Bible was put together over time.

Transforming congregations are places where people connect with their innermost being, with the Spirit that resides within. They are places where they can ask large questions and explore the mystery of God. They are places where people discover their vocation and purpose, where they can remember who they are trying to become. Transforming congregations are places where people learn to love God with all their mind, heart, and will and to connect to the powerful currents of Spirit that enliven them, teach them, and guide them forward.

QUESTIONS FOR REFLECTION

1. Draw a life map as suggested in Appendix D. Looking back
    over your life, what is one time you left behind a former version
    of yourself? What caused you to grow and change?

2. Who or what helped you construct a healthy ego? Was there
    ever a time when you relinquished that ego to a higher purpose?
    What happened?

3. What opportunities does your congregation provide for people
    to grow spiritually?

4. What else might your congregation do to create an environment
    that challenges people to grow?

1. attending college
   Religion classes — deeper understanding.

2. Junior high hist. teacher and all
   my music instructors — solo work
   both instrument & voice.
   Membership in symphony orch. while
   still in H.S.
   Learned to really listen to blend.

3. Bible studies, Helping Hands, Family
   Promise, Quilting, Circle.

4. We are all studying ~~Start~~ Thrive
   and we are having talking circles.
   This gives more of a sense of
   working together.

Connecting With Purpose

SPIRITUAL HABIT 4
ALIGNING

There's a thread you follow.
It goes among things that change. But it doesn't change.
People wonder about what you are pursuing.
You have to explain about the thread. [50]

– William Stafford

Two weeks before Christmas each year, my grandma announced it was time to make tamales. She went out on the back porch to collect the corn husks that had been drying since the end of summer. She went down to the cellar to retrieve the big pot my great grandmother had used to boil laundry. She went to the market to buy meat, corn meal, and dried hot peppers. For two days, the meat slowly simmered on the stove until it was so tender it fell off the bone.

Then it came time to assemble the kitchen crew. Grandma enlisted my mother to seed the peppers. She called on my aunt to grind the meat and the peppers together using the heavy iron grinder that was screwed on to one end of the counter. Meanwhile, she stirred the corn meal mush. When the mush was ready, she dished heaping mounds onto waxed paper laid out at each place around the kitchen table. My aunt put the big pan of the ground meat and peppers in the center. Then we all went to work on the rolling procedure: patting the corn meal mush flat on a corn husk, inserting the meat mixture, folding the husk over on three sides and tying the finished tamales into bundles with kite string. The process took all day.

While we rolled the tamales, we retold the story of how our German family had come to have a Mexican dish as its traditional holiday food. It all began when my great-grandfather lost his leg in an accident during the time he had worked for the railroad company. Back then, there was no such thing as disability insurance or workers' compensation so he and my great-grandmother had to find another way to make a living. When a traveling salesman came through town selling a recipe for tamales for fifty dollars, they dipped into their savings, bought the franchise, cooked up the food, and served it off a cart on the corner of Main Street. Two years later, they had made enough in profits to open a small restaurant.

Each year, my family did not just remember the tamale story; we re-enacted, lived it, and tasted it. Making tamales together became a habit in which we participated in a narrative from our family's tradition. Over the years, my grandma showed my mother and my aunt how to make the tamales, and my aunt and my mother showed me. The recipe was never written down. It was held in secret out of reverence for God (whom my family credited with sending the traveling salesman) and out of respect for my great-grandparents (who had risked everything in order to discover a new way to live.)

Each year, as we came around that kitchen table to roll tamales, to remember, and to re-live that story, we discovered all over again that we belonged to a people who did not give up, who trusted God to show them a way when there seemed to be no way at all. Participating in the story helped us remember who we were, what we stood for, and what we could become.

The story we live shapes our identity. Transforming congregations live a particular story that runs through the pages of scripture describing the reality of God's provision, peace, security, and justice for the world. That story fuels their imagination and orients them to a reality that exists in the already and the not-yet, in what is and what is to come. It provides a shared center for their life and ministry. It focuses their energy and helps them understand their purpose.

Some call that story the "Beloved Community." Others refer to it as "God's Reign" or "God's Dream for the World." A college student I once knew called it the "Really Real." Most translations of the Gospel of Matthew call it the "Kingdom of Heaven." The Gospels of Luke and Mark call it the "Kingdom of God." The prophet

Isaiah called it "God's New Creation." But, regardless of what name is used, it is a narrative that offers an image of the fullness of life.

GOD'S NEW CREATION

The story transforming congregations live begins at the beginning when God first gives form to what is a formless void. The first creation account tells how God separates light and darkness, day and night, land and sea, evening and morning, giving each aspect of creation its own clarity and purpose. The dome of the sky creates a safe place where life can thrive without being invaded by watery destruction.[51] That life is abundant; that life is good.[52] It includes trees yielding seeds in their fruit for food, winged birds, fish, cattle, creeping things, wild animals and human beings who are said to be the spitting image of the one who created them.

The first chapter of Genesis was written in a chaotic time of change when people had lost their bearings. They were living in a foreign land among strangers who practiced other religious traditions. All the rituals that had given their lives meaning and purpose back home had disappeared. They could no longer offer sacrifices at the temple in Jerusalem because that center of their spiritual lives had been destroyed. They could no longer look to the priests and the teachers of the law to give them leadership. They had to depend on the lay people among them to lead the community.

During that exile, they told each other stories as reminders of God's love and care for them. They remembered another time when they had wandered in the wilderness of Sinai. Each morning when the dew lifted, they had found a flaky substance, as fine as frost on the desert sand. "This is the bread God has given you to eat," Moses had told them. At the time, they had called it manna and later the psalmist poetically referred to it as the Bread of Angels.[53] For forty years that bread had provided enough nourishment to sustain their whole nation.

But there was a catch: the people were only to gather one measure of manna per person per day. If they got greedy and hoarded more than their fair share, the bread cultivated worms and became foul.[54] As it turned out, collecting bread morning by morning was not so much about obtaining food; it was about developing new spiritual habits and practicing a new way of life that offered sufficiency for all and freedom from the addiction of craving more. By collecting daily bread, the people learned to trust the provision of God.

As the prophets reflected on the experience of the Israelites in the desert, they imagined a time when the whole world would come to rely on that provision. On that day, not only would nations live in peace and security, but their work would have meaning. Isaiah shared the daring new vision:

> *They shall build houses and inhabit them;*
> *   they shall plant vineyards and eat their fruit.*
> *They shall not build and another inhabit;*
> *   they shall not plant and another eat;*
> *for like the days of a tree*
> *   shall the days of my people be,*
> *   and my chosen shall long enjoy*
> *   the work of their hands.*
> *They shall not labor in vain or bear children for*
> *   calamity, for they shall be the offspring blessed by the Lord*
> *   – and their descendants as well.*
> *Before they call I will answer,*
> *   while they are yet speaking I will hear.*
> *The wolf and the lamb shall feed together*
> *   and the lion shall eat straw like the ox.*

(Isaiah 65:21-25a)

On that day, death and destruction, anxiety and fear would all be wiped away. People would share such an intimate connection with God that they would hardly open their mouths to ask for what they needed before God would answer them. They would harvest the fruits of their labors and see that what they did mattered. They would live without fear of calamity. The prophet Micah could see that when that dream became reality, there would be no need of weapons because war would be no more:

They shall beat their swords into plowshares
and their spears into pruning hooks;
nation shall not lift up sword against nation.
neither shall they learn war any more;
but they shall all sit under their own vines
and under their own fig trees
and no one shall make them afraid. (Micah 4:3b-4a)

Physical violence would cease, armed conflict would be a thing of the past, and each person would have sufficient shelter and food.

Isaiah imagined the completion of God's intention for the world as a great big dinner party where everyone would accept God's invitation to feast. At God's table, each person would have a seat. Isaiah prophesized:

On this mountain, the Lord of hosts will make for all peoples
a feast of rich food, a feast of well-aged wines
of rich food filled with marrow
of well-aged wines strained clear. (Isaiah 25:6)

At God's table, all people would have their physical needs met and they would have a place where they could live free from fear. Around that table, they could be safe from physical violence, instability and insecurity. At God's table, all people would have a place where they belonged, where they were loved, recognized, and respected.

Many centuries later, Jesus re-appropriated that same vision. When he came to Galilee, he simply announced that God's intention for creation had come to pass. He declared that God's good provision for the fullness of life was available as a gift to all, even amid the chaos of the world. "The time is fulfilled," he said, "and the kingdom of God has come near; repent and believe in the good news."[55] Why wait for the end of time? Why not live in the present as *if* God's New Creation already had become a reality? Wouldn't living out of that dream, even in small ways, actually help to bring it about?

THE FIRST CHRISTIANS

As Jesus' followers practiced living God's New Creation and looked at the faces of those who gathered around the table each week, they saw the beginnings of God's New Creation made real. They discerned the ways God was blessing the poor in spirit, comforting those who mourned, giving the earth as an inheritance to the meek, filling those who were hungry and thirsty for what was right and just and good.[56] As they met week by week, they began to understand the power of God was accessible to them through prayer. They began to realize that bread blessed, broken, and shared could become a miracle of abundance for the whole world.[57]

Living as citizens of God's realm gave early followers a vantage point from which they could see clearly the injustice that permeated the political, social, and economic world of Rome. Living in both the kingdom of God and the kingdom of Caesar, they could discern the gaps between the two. They could see how the structures of the empire were favoring the rich and oppressing the landless tenant farmers. They could see how Rome's military power was thwarting God's peace and freedom. They could see how abundance for a few was preventing abundance for all.

Those first followers gathered around Jesus' table in order to be shaped by the values embedded in the story of God's New Creation. They came together to be equipped with the tools and the courage necessary to make God's intentions real. Although not large in number, the small bands that followed Jesus began to affect the whole fabric of the culture around them. They were like grains of mustard seed springing up like bushes everywhere. They were like leaven affecting the whole loaf, like salt flavoring the whole pot of soup. They were like light shining from a lamp stand showing what God had in mind for the world.

Early Christians experienced Jesus' presence with them, even after his execution. That presence taught them that they had nothing to fear. Through Jesus, God had swallowed up even death.[58] Now nothing was outside of God's realm and nothing could separate them from God's love.[59] That knowledge gave them the courage they needed to let go of their fear even in the face of hardship, hatred, persecution, hunger, danger, or violence. They could trust God in all the circumstances of their lives, even in death.

Each week, when they broke bread together, they met the Living Christ. Each week they went out from the table to participate in God's work of bringing life where there was death, freedom where there was captivity, and connection where there was alienation. They saw the Living Christ in the stranger who was hungry, thirsty, naked, sick, or imprisoned.[60] They reached out to those in need as ambassadors for Christ with a message of God's reconciling love.[61]

Today, as transforming congregations begin to talk about the kind of values they want to serve, they ask, "What would Jesus do?" and "How would he do it?" When they observe how Jesus honored all people regardless of status or gender, they too begin to claim the value of *respect*. When they hear how Jesus gathered a diversity of people as equals around the table, they begin to value *mutuality* as well. When they notice how Jesus crossed over social boundaries to gather all kinds of people around the table, they also begin to value *community*.

THE SPIRITUAL HABIT OF ALIGNING

God's New Creation offers a vision of the way things ought to be and invites the church to participate in creating that new world. As transforming congregations enter into God's New Creation through preaching and teaching, prayer and discernment, they align their purpose with God's purpose of peace, security, and justice for all. That purpose serves as common ground where people from a variety of backgrounds can form community and discover the work they are gifted to do in the world. It allows transforming congregations both to claim their Christian identity and to dialogue and partner with people of other religions and of no religion at all who want the world to be different.

Family Promise is one such organization that creates networks of Jewish, Muslim, and Christian congregations and volunteers who meet homeless families' immediate needs for shelter, meals, and comprehensive support services through the Interfaith Hospitality Network.[62] They also sponsor Voices Uniting where people of many faith traditions join together to alleviate poverty and improve the well-being of low-income families.

God's New Creation provides an alternative to the chronically dissatisfied existence the consumer culture sells. Where acquiring power and riches is a zero-sum game in the consumer culture, in the story of God's New Creation bread shared is bread multiplied. Where control, coercion and domination are the way to access power in the consumer culture, in the story surrender to an unseen mystery is the way to connect with true power. Where escape is touted as the path to security in the consumer culture, in the story, engagement in the messiness of the world is the way to insure the future.

That means living the story of God's New Creation also sets transforming congregations at odds with those outside the church who subscribe to a different set of values. Because God's New Creation redistributes power, giving a voice and a seat at the table to those on the margins, those who live that vision often discover they are in conflict with those who benefit from maintaining the status quo. The powerful resist being brought down so the lowly can be lifted up; the rich resist being sent away empty so the hungry can be filled.[63] Aligning with God's vision for the world requires courage because that vision creates not only a new order for the church, but a reordered world in which justice instead of status reigns.

CREATING A VISION STATEMENT

By living the story of God's New Creation, transforming congregations learn to set aside their own personal preferences and to find their purpose within God's purpose for creation. Certainly, one local church cannot share in all of what God is doing in the world; so transforming congregations must discern which part of God's vision will shape their ministry. It takes time. One group of leaders in Seattle prayed together for two years before naming the vision to which they believed God was calling them. Another congregation met in small groups for a year to discern what God was asking of them.

However long it lasts, several steps characterize the period of discernment in which a transforming congregation seeks to uncover God's vision for its life and ministry. Together the church:

1. **Immerses itself in the story of God's New Creation** in order to see what God is up to in the world.
2. **Relinquishes personal preference** as a criterion for decision-making in the church.
3. **Identifies one aspect of God's New Creation** which captures the congregation's imagination and stirs up its hope.
4. **Considers the particular personality, history, and location of the congregation** in order to name the congregation's gifts that make up its character.
5. **Writes a vision statement** that names what the congregation believes God is calling it to become.

Like God's New Creation, a vision statement is an acknowledgement of the already and the not yet, of who the congregation is and what it is to become. It must be big enough to challenge, but specific enough to focus the work of the church. Here are some examples of vision statements discerned by transforming congregations:

- *Living God's peace through dialogue, non-violence and advocacy*
- *Standing with the poor, the disenfranchised, and the outcast in order to insure basic security for all*
- *We serve a gracious God by creating a safe place where there is no need to fear*
- *To be an inclusive people living God's radical love that challenges all to grow in faith and mission*
- *Seeking the justice that makes peace possible*

It is not easy to discern the purpose of the church within God's larger purpose for the world; yet when a transforming congregation does that work, the vision allows it to steer a steady course. When individuals in the church voice their displeasure, the vision helps the congregation remain accountable to the decisions it has made

together. When various priorities vie for attention, the vision becomes the criteria by which the church evaluates every decision,
every project proposal, and every new hire. The church's vision
makes it possible to continue moving forward, even in the midst
of anxiety and confusion.

QUESTIONS FOR REFLECTION

1. Where do you see the story of God's New Creation being lived
   out today?

2. What part of God's purpose most captures your congregation's
   imagination?

3. What gifts are present in your congregation that could serve
   God's purposes in the world?

4. What is God's vision for your congregation?

Spiritual Habit 5
Engaging

All actual life is encounter[64]

– Martin Buber

When I was in the fourth grade, the congregation where I was a member held a School of Missions. It was a weeklong event that began each evening in the fellowship hall with unusual foods I had not tasted before such as curried rice, pad Thai, and pupusas. After supper, we went to our classrooms to learn about the mission work in the country whose food we had tasted. On the first night when I attended my class, my teacher gave me an offering box. He told me that the coins I put in there would support our missionaries—those especially dedicated individuals called by God and sent by the church into foreign lands.

Every once in a while, those foreign missionaries would visit the congregation, telling tales of difficult living conditions and cultural challenges they had encountered while trying to share the good news of Jesus Christ in some exotic location. Some were doctors who brought healing to those who were sick. Some were teachers who helped young people learn and grow. Some were engineers who helped villages dig wells and install sewer systems. Some were evangelists who established new churches.

I remember listening to their presentations, being impressed by their stories, and feeling just a little bit glad that they would be returning to the dangers of the mission field while I would go back to putting my change in the offering box in the safety of my own home. Of course, I was not the only one who took comfort in being able to leave the mission work to the professionals; in those days, most members of historic Protestant churches were content to offer their monetary support and prayers for others who would travel to the mission field, out there, over there, while they stayed within the familiar circle of congregational life.

Yet transforming congregations do not just play a supportive role in the mission of the church; they actively participate in that mission. They see that the mission field of the 21st Century begins at the church's doorstep and stretches out into the neighborhood and into an interconnected, interdependent world. They understand themselves to be the missionaries who are called and sent, ready or not, to engage in making real God's New Creation.

THE MISSIONAL CHURCH

Luke's Gospel told how Jesus appointed seventy people and sent them on ahead of him in pairs to every town and place where he himself intended to go. He said to them, "Carry no purse, no bag. Wear no sandals."[65] They were to dress like beggars but they were not to beg. Instead, they were to get acquainted with strangers by eating and drinking with them, by building relationships with them over time.

To be in mission is to become friends with neighbors, to accompany them through times of trial and critical need. The root of that word accompaniment is com which means "with" and pan which means "bread." So walking with neighbors is really about sharing bread together—about "being with" more than "doing for." Sometimes "walking with" involves risking personal comfort and security in order to come alongside others who are struggling. Yet transforming congregations discover that the times they find the courage to move through the discomfort of accompanying others in their suffering are also the times when they learn the most about themselves, when they grow exponentially in faith, and when they find new energy, new vitality.

For one congregation in California, it was a matter of getting on the other side of the counter. The church had been serving a meal on a weeknight to people in the neighborhood, many who had no home. Those in the congregation happily cooked the meal in the kitchen, and served the meal from the kitchen. But they only learned what it meant to "walk with" when they came out of the kitchen into the fellowship hall to eat dinner with their guests.

Now they operate on a buddy system in which each person from the congregation makes sure they check in at the meal with one or more people from the neighborhood. Sometimes they start up a card game before dinner. In that setting, conversation comes more naturally. Sometimes they offer art materials where those who may not feel comfortable conversing about their week can express themselves through paint or pastels. Always, they look for ways to connect, not as counselors, but as friends who care about each other's lives. The conversations not only provide an extra safety net for those who may be at risk, but they continue to change those who used to serve the meal from behind the counter.

THE SPIRITUAL HABIT OF ENGAGING

In his farewell remarks in the Gospel of John, Jesus promised the disciples that the Spirit of Truth would guide them into all the truth.[66] If they chose to live in the Spirit, they would be able to access God's wisdom and the Spirit would teach them all that they needed to know.[67] If they connected to the Spirit, their perception would enlarge. They would be able to see with the eyes of God and would discern wise action as they lived out their roles as prophets, teachers, healers, and organizers.[68]

The Spirit reveals the unvarnished reality of how things are,[69] holding up a mirror that allows us to see who we are without pretense. It shows us both our giftedness and our human limits. When we hear a message that seems to resonate, causing a "yes" to well up from deep within, we know we are tapping into the truth of the Spirit. However, the Spirit does not just show who we are, it also allows us to see the truth of the world in which we live. It opens our eyes to both the precious beauty of life and the pain and suffering it brings. "Those who are spiritual are able to discern all things,"[70] the Apostle Paul wrote to the church at Corinth, and that discernment highlights the breach between God's vision of wholeness and the reality of brokenness around us. Through the Spirit we receive knowledge and that knowledge can break our hearts. (See Appendix E for a chart you can use to assess where there is a gap between the already and the not-yet of God's New Creation in your own context of ministry.)

Standing in the breach between the beautiful possibilities of the world and the reality of suffering, hate, and death can bring us to despair. Yet when that despair causes us to give up our own pride, to admit that by our own power we cannot change things, then the Spirit is most able to do its work. "Not by might, nor by power, but by my spirit,"[71] God told the prophet Zechariah. The Spirit that lives within us can lead us, guide us, and help us in our times of weakness, but only if we are willing to humble ourselves in the manner of Jesus who

> *though he was in the form of God*
> *did not regard equality with God*
> *as something to be exploited*
> *but emptied himself,*
> *taking on the form of a slave.*   (Philippians 2:6-8)

When transforming congregations empty themselves—or as Alcoholics Anonymous might say, when they "surrender" to their Higher Power—they are most able to connect with the source of creative love. When they give up control, they find their greatest freedom. When they give up striving for their own survival, they discover a grace they simply may have for free. When they pray like Jesus, "Not my will but yours be done,"[72] they began to experience new life.

Most transforming congregations can point to one or two pivotal moments in their history when they released their will to the will of God, humbled themselves, gave up the pursuit of their own agenda, and opened themselves up to the unknown. Those moments often came when they stood between the old way of doing things that no longer worked and the way forward that they could not see. "We had to get to the place where we had nothing left to lose before we were willing to give up our own agenda and really start listening for what God wanted from us," one pastor said to me. Another woman put it this way: "We just sort of let go when our congregation hit bottom. We didn't know what to do anymore; we didn't even know what to try. And that's when things began to change."

One congregation in Washington was ready to close its doors when the local shelter came to ask if they could use the church basement to create more overnight housing for those living on the streets. The congregation once had been very protective of its building, but when worship attendance got down to a small handful of faithful souls, the church decided to let its building be used by those in need. "Now we have a vital ministry that is making a difference in our community," they said, "and our church is starting to grow again."

Once transforming congregations release their will to the will of God, then they are free to ask the question, "Who is my neighbor?" Like foreign missionaries sent into a new culture, they begin by noticing what is going on.

- Who shops in the stores?
- Who lives in the neighborhood? Are they families with young children or teens or mostly empty-nesters?
- What is the socio-economic status of the neighborhood? Are people rich or middle class or poor? Does it appear the housing is mostly rentals or do residents own their own homes?
- What is the racial and ethnic make-up of the neighborhood?
- Where do people gather? What do they do for fun?

Some congregations use demographic studies or census data to help them get answers to those questions. Some just play detective themselves by walking around the community and making observations. What businesses are in the area? Are there social service agencies present? Are there schools or medical facilities? The languages of the signs on businesses provide information about the background of the residents. The number of mailboxes serves as a clue about whether a house has been subdivided into apartments for rent. The kinds of parked cars hint at the socio-economic status of those who drive them. Children's toys out in yards signal that young families are present. It is amazing what a church can learn just by looking.[73]

Next, transforming congregations get acquainted with those who live in their community. They write down a few questions they want to ask and they practice asking those questions of each other. Then, like the disciples Jesus called and sent, they go out in pairs to listen to store clerks, servers in restaurants, business owners, social service workers, government officials, school principals, and health care providers.

- What do you like about living here?
- What are your concerns about this community?
- What keeps you up at night?
- What is this neighborhood's greatest need?"

They find that many neighborhood residents worry about those trying to shake addictions, those with mental or physical disabilities, those who are engaged in crime. They care about those who suffer broken relationships and broken dreams. They are concerned about those who live in poverty or loneliness, who are looking for a way to make their lives count for something. (See Appendix H for a guide to asking Open and Honest questions.)

In conducting the interviews, transforming congregations make use of a practice called "contemplative listening" when engaging their neighbors. They still the chatter in their own minds so they are able to focus completely on what is being said. Instead of playing back what they heard (as is the practice in active listening), they simply receive what they hear without comment. When transforming congregations listen contemplatively, they discover that people in their neighborhood are hungry for hope and the fullness of life.

As transforming congregations build relationships with their neighbors and listen to their stories they begin to get new insight into the ways the world has changed. Through their explorations, some uncover the economic poverty which had been invisible to them before. Some expose the poverty of soul perpetrated by the rampant materialism of the consumer culture. Some find the poverty of community that exists in spite of the growing use of high speed networking.

How can the church serve those needs? As transforming congregations try to answer that question, they do not just gather as a church. Right from the start, they invite those they interviewed to be part of the process. They check out their own perceptions with their neighbors. Together they dialogue and evaluate their data in order to decide on a common focus for their mission. Together they set goals—not for the congregation alone—but with an eye to the kind of transformation they hope to see in the lives of people in the neighborhood when their mission is accomplished.

How transforming congregations choose to engage in mission depends on the resources available to them, the gifts of their participants, and the context in which they do their ministries. Engagement by each church in each neighborhood looks a little different. Some of the many ways transforming congregations carry out their mission include:

1. INCARNATIONAL MINISTRY: A group commits to live in one neighborhood, to build relationships in that neighborhood, to share meals and prayer together, and to live Jesus' values through their vocational and social lives.

2. SMORGASBORD MINISTRY: In larger congregations, pairs of leaders commit for one year to coordinate a particular mission in the neighborhood, such as tutoring children, picking up trash, or building houses. People both inside and outside the congregation who want to participate in those ministries connect electronically with those leaders in order to be scheduled to serve.

3. ORGANIZING MINISTRY: Once a congregation has identified a need in the community by listening to its neighbors, church leaders gather agencies, organizations, and other churches to coordinate efforts. Together they focus on how they can meet that need and change their community. They ask a question such as, "How can we work together to lower the school drop-out rate in our community?"

4. FILL-THE-GAP MINISTRY: Individuals within a congregation interview neighbors such as business owners, health care providers, school personnel, or social workers to determine the greatest needs in the community. Then the church develops a strategic plan to address the needs not being met. Eventually a fill-the-gap ministry may even become its own non-profit organization.

5. GRANT-GIVING MINISTRY: Congregations with substantial monetary resources create a grant-giving ministry. They might give start-up money to ministries that are doing effective missional work or they might actually develop a grant application process in order to fund other people's good ideas that hold promise for giving people a hand up.

6. INSIDE-OUT MINISTRY: Congregations that discover they have individuals inside the congregation who could benefit from a ministry, such as grief recovery, job-hunting support, or money management form a small group with an equal number of individuals outside the congregation who also are in need of that ministry. They reach those people by advertising and creating a registration process.

7. BUILDING MINISTRY: A congregation with a large facility invites other non-profit organizations or churches to use their space for free or for a minimal cost.

8. MOBILIZING MINISTRY: Leaders of a congregation recruit teams of people to participate in community fundraising efforts, vigils for peace and justice, lobbying efforts, local mission projects, or mission trips. Others provide the organizational leadership for those events and the church sends the participants.

9. SHADOW MINISTRY: Individuals who participate in a congregation start a ministry with those who have been wounded by an experience of church in the past. The congregation's name does not appear as a sponsor of the ministry even though the church might provide funds and leadership to support the ministry.

10. SYSTEMIC MINISTRY: A congregation partners with other churches or organizations which care about a specific need to influence elected officials or others who have power to create systemic change that serves the values of God's New Creation.

In one neighborhood, a group of churches got together to start a free clinic for those who did not have access to health care. Another group of churches got together to provide shelter and food for teenagers living on the street. Seeing that poor women had little collateral that would make them eligible for bank loans, one church worked with other non-profits to establish a micro-loan service for small start-up businesses in their community. Another faith community worked with the city to provide low income housing for those who could not afford to pay rent. Another congregation sponsored a job fair in order to connect people who were out of work with expanded opportunities for employment.

However transforming congregations choose to walk with their neighbors, engaging in mission provides an entry point for newcomers. Researcher and historian, Diana Butler Bass, notes that those who have left the church or those who have never been part of a faith community may not be interested in "joining" the church, but they may be very interested in "joining in" to make a difference in the lives of people in the community with their time, money, or expertise.[74]

CREATING A STRATEGIC MINISTRY PLAN

Transforming congregations turn outward to the needs of the world rather than inward to their own survival. They create a Strategic Ministry Plan that involves the following movements:

- **Seeing** the needs of people in their geographic area
- **Reflecting** on the root causes of those needs and what the Spirit might lead them to do to about those needs
- **Connecting** with neighbors to discover what is already being done and/or how partnerships might be formed
- **Choosing** a strategic action to address a need
- **Carrying** out the action

- **Evaluating** the action in order to learn from it
- **Celebrating** what was accomplished through the action

To arrive at a strategic missional plan which includes a purpose, a vision, goals, and action steps designed to reach those goals, they may ask these questions which also may be found in Appendix F:

- What purpose and values will we serve in our mission?
- What is the current reality in the neighborhood?
- What changes most need to take place in our neighborhood for it to more closely resemble God's New Creation?
- Who are the individuals and organizations that are already working to make those changes?
- What do those individuals and organizations have to teach us?
- What gifts do we have in our congregation that could be used to further God's work in the world?
- Who might partner with us in accomplishing that work?
- How will we fund this ministry?
- What shall we do first?
- When will we evaluate the results of that action in order to decide what we should do next?

Once transforming congregations decide what to do, they get organized to accomplish that work. Along the way, they often modify their strategic plan as new situations arise that require flexibility and creativity. When a step in the strategic plan is completed, they celebrate what they have achieved with their partners and tell the story widely through media available to them.

One congregation decided to plant street trees in their neighborhood. They worked with the city government that purchased the trees. They worked with a local nursery to help them learn how to plant the trees. They researched residents in the community who had made a difference in the lives of others, and they enlisted the help of a local artist to create named plaques to honor those residents. One Saturday congregational participants put the trees in the ground and placed a plaque in front of each tree. Then they held a neighborhood block party and distributed short biographies of the people named on the plaques.

Transforming congregations discover that creating a missional plan renews their energy because it helps them focus on participating in something larger than their own self-interests. It provides renewed joy that comes from rediscovering their vocation as those called and sent to act with courage and compassion. It delivers renewed meaning that comes from becoming a church that matters. It supplies renewed hope as the congregation receives gifts from those who once were strangers and now are friends.

QUESTIONS FOR REFLECTION

1. When have you engaged in mission? What did that experience mean to you?

2. Why might a relational mission of "being with" rather than "doing for" be difficult for some North Americans?

3. What criteria will you use to help you evaluate whether a mission has been successful or not?

4. What steps will you take in order to identify a missional focus for your congregation?

SPIRITUAL HABIT 6
TESTIFYING

We cannot hold it in our hands and put it on a scale,
but we feel the weight, the force, of its influence in our lives.
We cannot hear it, but we hear ourselves speaking and singing
and testifying because it moves, inspires and directs us to do so.[75]
— Gloria Wade-Gayles

The church was having a car wash on a Saturday morning to raise funds for those who had been displaced from their homes by some nearby wildfires. My husband and I had read about the church and had followed the blogs of one of the congregation's leaders before we came to visit. We had planned to worship with the congregation the next day, but our car was plenty dirty so we drove to the church parking lot that morning.

Those who were washing cars saw our bumper sticker right away. "Oh, you're Disciples!" they said. We told them we lived in Montana. "Well, what are you doing here?" they asked.

"We came to see you," my husband said. "We're pastors traveling on sabbatical. We're visiting churches that have a reputation for reaching out to their neighbors."

"Well, that's us!" they said. Then they each introduced themselves.

"You know, our pastor left a few months ago to go serve another church," they told us. "We don't even have an interim minister yet."

"Yes," we said, "we know." Actually, we had put the church on our list of places to visit just to observe how the congregation was functioning without the strong leadership of their founding minister.

"What did your pastor do to prepare you for her departure?" my husband asked.

"Oh, it was God who prepared us," they said without hesitation. "Over the last few years, God sent us just the right people with the gifts we would need. Now, we have a great team in place who preach, lead our ministries, and share their musical talents with us on Sunday morning. Everyone's pitching in."

They started in on our car, so we walked around the property. In the vacant lot next to the modest church building, we saw signs of a community garden being built in conjunction with a housing development next door. Inside the church, we were greeted with a bulletin board entitled "God's Miracles Every Day." It was full of pictures and news clippings telling stories of the miracles that had happened because of the church's ministries. We read about the congregation giving away prayer shawls, collecting school supplies, setting up a booth at the Pride Festival, and volunteering at a free dental clinic at the fair.

On the fellowship hall wall a banner announced the church's identity statement: We cultivate love that is greater than our differences. Beneath that were the congregation's areas of focus: Building Relationships; Nurturing Youth; Mission Outreach; Shared Story. Along one wall a sign invited people to take a piece of paper and write down their prayers, thoughts, worries, or thanksgivings and attach them to a large cross.

Back outside, I asked one younger woman who was scrubbing away at our car, "Why do you belong to this congregation?"

"This church is not based in fear," she said, "but on how you can become the person God created you to be."

"We are a lot of people recovering from bad church experiences," another woman chimed in. "I bounced around for five years from church to church before landing here. I just couldn't swallow the fundamentalism those other congregations were dishing out."

Like a lot of the vital congregations we visited on sabbatical, that transforming congregation was clear about its character as a church. It was able to communicate its identity clearly and succinctly—even at a Saturday morning car wash! It was not shy about talking out loud about the ways it experienced the power and presence of God in and through its life and work in the community.

WE ARE A PEOPLE WHO

In a court of law, witnesses testify to what they have seen and heard. Testimony cannot be hearsay; it must arise out of personal experience. It must be the truth, the whole truth, and nothing but the truth. In the life of the church, testimony is the clear articulation of how the character of the congregation has been shaped by the Spirit's transforming activity. Individuals testify when they tell how the Spirit has empowered them, encouraged them, or enlivened them in times of trial; but the whole community also gives testimony through writing, artistic expression, preaching, teaching, and singing. When the church testifies, it tells the truth about who it has become and is becoming in relation to the holy presence of God that is active in the midst of the congregation's life and ministry.

The identity of the people of Israel came from the *Shema*: "Hear, O Israel: The Lord is our God, the Lord alone. You shall love the Lord your God with all your heart, and with all your soul, and with all your might" (Deuteronomy 6:4-5). That testimony not only reminded them of the character of God, but it shaped their vision, mission, and values as a people.

To make the words of the *Shema* more than words, the Israelites recited them to their children. They proclaimed them when they came together as a community. They talked about them when they were at home and when they were away. They put the *Shema* inside a little container called a *mezuzah* which they attached to the doorposts of their houses. They touched the *mezuzahs* each time they came and went to remind themselves what they were to be about. Some even bound the words onto their arms or attached them to a headband so they would never forget who they were called to be.

Each year, during the Passover, the Israelites told how God had led them as a people out of Egypt. But they did not just recount those events as if they happened to past generations; they described them as if they were personal experiences. "*We* were Pharaoh's slaves in Egypt but the Lord brought *us* out of Egypt with a mighty

hand" (Deteronomy 6:21, *emphasis* added). In the telling, time
was eclipsed. The ancient story became their own. As they testified
to God's marvelous deeds of freeing, guiding, and feeding their
ancestors, they discovered those same events happening in their
current context. As they recalled the story of the Exodus, they remembered they too were a people who had been set free. Testimony
does not just help a community remember the past; it also helps
that community claim who it is in the present.

Jesus testified to his own purpose and identity using the same
words Isaiah used in describing God's call:

> *The spirit of the Lord is upon me;*
> *because he has anointed me*
> *   to bring good news to the poor.*
> *He has sent me to proclaim release to the captives*
> *   and recovery of sight to the blind*
> *   to let the oppressed go free,*
> *to proclaim the year of the Lord's favor."*   (Luke 4:18)

In that moment, Jesus made it clear that he would not pursue
his own self-interests. With his own heart tuned with the heart of
God, he would offer a new way of seeing for the blind, freedom
for those in bondage, and joy for those seeking healing, wholeness
and justice for all creation.

Several months later, John the Baptist sent his disciples to ask
Jesus a question: "Are you the one who is to come, or are we to wait
for another?"[76] John had been imprisoned, he was facing his own
death, and he had begun to doubt Jesus' identity. In response Jesus
said, "Go and tell John what you hear and see: the blind receive
their sight, the lame walk, the lepers are cleansed, the deaf hear, the
dead are raised, and the poor have good news brought to them."[77]
He instructed John's disciples to give testimony to deeds that could
be seen, heard, and told that provided evidence of God's activity
in the world, that embodied Jesus' identity and purpose, and that
could revive John's trust in God.

When Jesus knew he would not be around much longer, he
talked to his own disciples about how to hold fast to the way he

had taught them to live. "I have said these things to you while I am still with you," he told them, "but the Advocate, the Holy Spirit … will teach you everything and remind you of all that I have said to you."[78] Jesus told them that the Advocate would testify on his behalf and that the disciples also were to testify to what they had seen and heard while they were with him.[79]

Later, Peter and John did just that on the Solomon's Portico on the east side of the Temple. In response to their testimony, the religious leaders tried to silence them by threatening arrest. But Peter and John answered them, "Whether it is right in God's sight to listen to you rather than to God, you must judge; for we cannot keep from speaking about what we have seen and heard."[80] When the Spirit, moves, inspires and directs testimony, it is almost impossible to remain silent.

THE SPIRITUAL HABIT OF TESTIFYING

In transforming congregations, testimony does not emerge out of obligation; it spills out from genuine excitement about the ways God is acting in and through the ministry of the church. Transforming congregations offer witness in their one-on-one encounters with other people. The sound of animated conversation fills the air before worship as people talk about where they have met God during the week, as they share good news about ministry that has taken place, and as they share stories about the ways the Spirit has been transforming the lives of individuals in the neighborhood.

Inside the church, anniversaries become occasions when people, touched by the care of the church, give testimony. Stewardship drives become times for talking about lives transformed by the ways the church used its resources in mission. Worship services allow for moments of thanksgiving when individuals can share how God worked in their lives because of the relationships they built in and through the church.

In one congregation, Jeff rose to tell how the prayer shawl the congregation made for him became his security blanket during the many treatments for cancer he had to undergo. In another, Dottie shared how the twelve-step program that met in the church gave her a whole new life. In another, Judith talked about how she experienced the guidance of the Spirit through the church's small group ministry.

Beyond the church walls, transforming congregations testify when they are with other congregations, when they are in small groups, and when they are around dinner tables. They give testimony through social media and on blogs about how God is changing their lives. They tell stories about their encounters with the holy in a matter-of-fact way, without embarrassment, apology, or even much explanation. Transforming congregations perceive that the Spirit is active in their lives and they are not ashamed to say so.

Transforming congregations move their vision, mission and core values from the head to the heart, not by tucking those words away in a file drawer, but by publicly and frequently proclaiming them as the essence of the church's identity. They preach them and teach them. They display them on websites, on projection screens, in bulletins, and on brochures. Many stencil them on their walls as reminders of their identity.

Above each doorway and window in the fellowship hall of a church in California you can read these words: "Creativity, Healing, Hospitality, Honoring the Body, Peacemaking, Keeping Sabbath, Mindful Consuming, Deep Listening, and Loving Speech." A banner graces the front of the space where an Oregon church gathers: "Sharing Good News with the Poor." That same church invites the congregation to recite their identity statement as part of the call to worship each week: "Today we gather as a community dedicated to justice, peace, and the way of Jesus." The newsletter of a church in Washington reminds the congregation each month about their identity: "We are a church with a welcoming spirit, a heart for children, and the desire to grow and deepen our faith."

Individuals in transforming congregations often carry home mementos to help them recall who they are trying to become. They tape lines from sermons, Bible verses or quotations to their bathroom mirrors. They include a phrase from a poem or song as a by-line in an email as a way of reminding themselves of the values they are trying to live. They create little altars in their homes with candles, photographs, and bits of nature to remind them of their place in creation and in the larger story of God's New Creation.

One church uses the occasion of All Saints Day to testify to the lives of people who have been part of the congregation down through the years who lived Jesus' values in spite of pressures to do otherwise. As they tell each story, they give a different shaped bead to each child present. The children string the beads onto bracelets that they wear home to remind them of the kind of community to which they belong.

But testimony does not just stem from the stories of people in the congregation; transforming congregations often testify to the activity of God by sharing biographies of people in the history of the church or in the life of the world who have served the values Jesus served. They tell the stories of people from the Christian tradition that lived those values. Sometimes they even go on a pilgrimage to live a piece of those stories such as traveling to Assisi to walk in the footsteps of Francis, traveling to El Salvador to see what Oscar Romero saw, traveling to Turkey to follow the routes of the Apostle Paul.

They also testify to the lives of ordinary people who do extraordinary things in God's name. They talk about those who rebuilt New Orleans after the hurricane and those who went to Indonesia to clean up after a tidal wave. They talk about women who built co-operative businesses in Croatia and companies who invented solar ovens so villagers would not have to gather wood from the precious rain forest in order to eat a hot dinner. Testimony is at the heart of what encourages those in transforming congregations; testimony gives them the courage they need for further growth, further risk.

Truthful testimony inspires those who hear it to be honest about their own lives. That is the genius of Alcoholics Anonymous. When people hear others telling the truth, they find the courage to confront the lies they have been telling themselves about themselves and to speak up about secrets they have been keeping. Many a pastor knows how one person's story opens the way for others in the congregation to tell their own truths. When one person admits to a drug addiction, his testimony allows others to confront their additions; when one person admits to being a closeted mystic, her testimony encourages others to talk about their intimate experiences of the Spirit.

When transforming congregations testify through the stories of the Bible, through formative stories from the congregation's history, through the biographies of those heroes and heroines who make up the surrounding cloud of witnesses,[81] and through stories from daily lives of people in the present, they bear witness to a God who breaks into human experience. Individual and corporate testimony shapes those congregations into brave communities that are able to hold fast to their identity even when other values vie for their allegiance.

QUESTIONS FOR REFLECTION

1. What is one story that has shaped your own identity or the identity of the congregation in which you participate?

2. On what occasions does the congregation in which you participate testify to how the Spirit acts in and through the ministry of the church?

3. How comfortable are you testifying about the Spirit's activity in your life?

4. How does your congregation publicly proclaim its common vision, mission and core values? Are there ways you could make the church's identity more visible?

Connecting with Community

SPIRITUAL HABIT 7
WELCOMING

The real host is the one
who offers space where we do not have to be afraid
and where we can listen to our own inner voice
and find our own personal way of being human.[82]
– Henry Nouwen

My cousin Rosemary had lots of children. Each time a new baby was born, she and her husband added a new room onto their tiny house in the country. Rosemary's kitchen table was made from a sheet of plywood perched on top of two homemade saw horses and covered by a red and white checked cloth. Around it was a conglomeration of mismatched chairs—enough so her whole family could gather around the table at one time.

It seemed like I always found myself in Rosemary's kitchen when I was facing some kind of difficulty in my own life. I would come through the back door and Rosemary would invite me to sit down at that table while she fixed me a sandwich. She believed any problem was better faced on a full stomach. While I ate, I talked and Rosemary listened.

I sat at Rosemary's table when I was twelve, feeling awkward and lonely because I didn't fit in with the popular students at school. I sat there when I was seventeen, wondering what kind of vocation I might pursue. I sat there when my marriage was falling apart, when my mother died, and when I didn't know where to turn. During those times, I don't remember Rosemary ever giving me advice or even offering an opinion about whatever was bothering me. She just gave me sandwiches and listened.

At Rosemary's table, I could be exactly who I was, without pretense. I could risk telling myself the truth about myself and I could speak that truth aloud without fear of criticism. At Rosemary's table, I knew that I had a place—that I was welcomed and loved and accepted, regardless of how unlovely I might be feeling. Inevitably, by the time I had finished my sandwich, I felt stronger and more confident that I could handle whatever life would dish out. Rosemary created the kind of trustworthy space every human being needs in order to do the hard work of growing up.

HOSPITALITY FOR THE SOUL

Hospitality for the soul is what I received at Rosemary's table. When I showed up in her kitchen, Rosemary did not comfort or confront me. She did not try to help me or fix me. She just created safe place where I could struggle with my own problems and access the wisdom of the Spirit. As a result, I found that I did not have to spend time protecting or defending my ego. I was free to be honest, to speak the truth about what I was experiencing, and to allow that inner Spirit to guide me.

Educator Parker Palmer reminds us just how rare hospitality for the soul is in today's world.

> In this culture, we know how to create spaces that invite the intellect to show up, to argue its case, to make its point. We know how to create spaces that invite the emotions to show up, to express anger or joy. We know how to create spaces that invite the will to show up, to consolidate effort and energy around a common task. And we surely know how to create spaces that invite the ego to show up, preening itself and claiming its turf! But we seem to know very little about creating spaces that invite the soul to show up, this core of ourselves, our selfhood.

The soul rarely risks being seen in threatening places. Criticism, judgment, and blame send the soul into hiding because they diminish the Self. The soul experiences welcome only when physical, psychological, and spiritual safety are present.

That kind of safety often is hard to find in a congregation. One of the top reasons people give for not participating in church is their experience of Christians as judgmental, mean, and critical.[83]

When they listen to the strident, divisive rhetoric that comes from Christian voices in the media and find those same voices present at church board meetings, they feel uncomfortable. When they express an opinion countered by theological bullies who question their faithfulness, they feel unsafe. When others judge them for their appearance, or for the way they lead, or for their taste in music, they simply ask "Who needs it?"[84]

Transforming congregations that want to offer welcome find they first must do some preliminary spiritual work. They begin that work by recognizing the fear of the stranger which has been installed from an early age. As children, we are taught to avoid conversations with people we do not know, to lock doors, and to watch our luggage in airports. We are warned that strangers can jeopardize our physical safety and take advantage of any vulnerability if we are not vigilant. *here*

To offer true hospitality, those who are part of the church find they must confront their natural distrust of those they do not know. That does not mean that they should act in stupid ways, naively assuming there is no such thing as a dangerous situation; but it does mean that they should confront barriers such as gender prejudice, cultural intolerance, racism, or age bias that they find within themselves which cause them to pre-judge strangers.

The second bit of interior work transforming congregations find they must do if they want to welcome others is to recognize their own neediness. A congregation who has a spoken or unspoken agenda for their guests cannot be truly hospitable. The church must first clear away all expectations about what guests can provide before it can create trustworthy space. If the congregation harbors the hope that newcomers will become replacement parts for congregational participants who are worn out from carrying the load of leadership, if it expects visitors to become part of the church in order to fill the void of grief and loneliness left by the church's decline, it cannot provide real welcome.

The third piece of interior work a transforming congregation must do to provide welcome is to admit that friendliness is not the same as welcome. In a friendly congregation, ushers smile and greet visitors with a handshake and a kind word; church participants introduce themselves during coffee time, and sometimes offer visitors bags of popcorn containing the note, "We're glad you popped in." In a friendly church, members learn the names of new families and make sure the children find their way to Christian education classes; old-timers sit with newcomers in worship, explaining the nuances of the service not clearly spelled out in the bulletin; afterwards, they invite visitors to mid-week activities or sign them up for jobs around the church.

As important as those acts of friendliness may be, they soon can become empty gestures if they are not followed by genuine hospitality that makes room for the gifts of the other. In one congregation, when younger newcomers began taking on leadership, the warmth with which they were initially greeted disappeared. The established members complained that the women who had more recently come to the congregation didn't comply with the rules of the church kitchen. Others grumbled about noisy, active children disrupting the Sunday service. When younger adults introduced a different kind of music, old-timers put up for it for a while, but soon grew angry about all the changes in the church. The atmosphere in the congregation grew tenser until the young people gave up and left. Then the old-timers breathed a sigh of relief and the church return to its comfortable former habits.

That church was friendly, but it certainly was not welcoming. Friendliness assimilates newcomers into what already exists; welcome integrates newcomers by helping them know they belong. Friendliness says, "We're glad you came to our table. We hope you feel at home here eating what we like to eat and doing things the way we like to do them." Welcome goes beyond friendliness to say, "We want you to bring your gifts to this community. We know when you offer those gifts that we will be changed by your presence among us."

MEALS OF MUTUALITY

Welcome shares power rather than keeping it in the hands of those who maintain the status quo. Never was that made more apparent than when the Apostle Paul confronted the behavior of Christians in Corinth. Growth in the church of the First Century caused some people to be excluded.[85] On the occasions when the small house congregations in Corinth gathered together at the villa of one of the more wealthy members of the community, only some guests could be accommodated inside the home in the 55 square meter dining hall called the *triclinium*; the rest were seated outside the home in the 36 square meter patio called the *atrium*. The *triclinium* contained couches where diners could recline while eating;[86] those in the *atrium* sat on straight-backed benches which lined the walls.[87]

But that is not where the discrimination ended. Hosts in the early church often followed the popular cultural practice of "elegant economy": setting the best dishes in front of a select few while serving cheap scraps to everyone else and pouring different grades of wine according to various "grades" of friends.[88] For Paul, treating people unequally was not just a matter of hurting a few people's feelings; creating an elite group went against the very identity of the church as Christ's body.[89]

Paul's letter to the church at Corinth reflected his anger:

> *When you come together, it is not really to eat the Lord's Supper. For when the time comes to eat, each of you goes ahead with your own supper, and one goes hungry and another becomes drunk. What! Do you not have homes to eat and drink in? Or do you show contempt for the church of God and humiliate those who have nothing?* (1 Corinthians 11:20-22a)

Visibly diverse, the community was to live out the invisible reality of its oneness. Any sense of entitlement or personal privilege was to be rejected. The inclusion of some at the expense of others went against the very nature of what it meant to follow Jesus.

Paul expected the Christians in Corinth to include all people at the table just as Jesus had done during his lifetime. Jesus' meals of mutuality stood in distinct contrast to those of the empire where inviting friends and clients to dine was a way for a patron to display his or her power and to wield control over the guests.[91]

At most Roman meals, guests actually were arranged around the table according to their standing in relation to the host. The most honored person usually was seated to the right of the one presiding at the meal.[92] Such a tribute often bought favors and pay-back was expected.[93] But in Jesus' circle, each person came as an equal. There were no seats of honor, no special privilege.

In Jesus' world, the holiness law code determined the degree of welcome one received within the Jewish religious community. In one respect, holiness was a matter of geography.[94] The code recognized that the holiest place in the world was the inner sanctum of the Jewish temple where only the priests were allowed to enter. The next best place related to holiness was the temple sanctuary, then the outer courts, beyond that the Temple Mount, the city of Jerusalem, and finally the land of Israel. Respectable people did not go beyond that boundary.

Holiness was also determined by birth and blood.[95] Priests and Levites inherited their privileged status through their ancestral lines. But if a person was not lucky enough to be born to the right people, he or she could always gain respect by observing the Jewish Law. Observant Jews were better than non-observant Jews. Those who *would* not keep the law out of choice—people like tax collectors and prostitutes—were still considered better than those who *could* not keep the law because of a physical condition—people like lepers, slaves, women, the blind, the lame, the deaf, and the insane. Observant Jews could lose their respectable status by associating with non-observant Jews. They were told to stay away from those who were bodily unclean or morally unclean.

By contrast, Jesus welcomed all. Where other righteous people stayed close to Jerusalem, Jesus traveled freely through Gentile country. Where the law defined some people as impure, Jesus crossed the boundaries of exclusion. Where other religious leaders did everything they could to remain ritually pure, Jesus violated religious tradition by putting the needs of people above the laws regarding food.[96] He healed a naked demoniac, touched lepers, took corpses by the hand, associated with women, the lame and the deaf, and called a tax collector to be one of his disciples. One time he even applied his own spit (an impure bodily fluid) to the eyes of a blind man. Jesus did not fear the stranger; he welcomed Gentiles and Jews, servants and free citizens, men and women, and rich and poor at his table, and integrated them into the life of the community.

THE SPIRITUAL HABIT OF WELCOME

Transforming congregations become inclusive communities by welcoming the stranger and forming mutual relationships. However, offering true hospitality to a wide range of people takes time and attention. The leaders of one congregation found it necessary to learn about "the culture of poverty" in order to better understand those from the neighborhood who were participating in the life of the church. In another congregation, participants educated themselves in the worship practices of the local Native American tribe in order to be more culturally attuned to their customs.

"We thought we were being an inclusive congregation," one lay leader told me, "but the visual effect of what we actually *looked like* spoke louder than our words. Members of the church were mostly white, mostly older, and mostly affluent. So ten years ago, we began to change. We called an African-American pastor. We began singing a variety of songs from all parts of the world in worship. We voted to be a congregation that was open and affirming of gay and lesbian people and began flying a rainbow flag outside our front door. We began ministries that put us in touch with people from other social strata. Now our congregation more resembles those who live right around the church building."

In transforming congregations, welcome is communicated by the music, language, and style of worship which reflect the sub-cultures of the neighborhood. Transforming congregations make sure the visual images displayed in the building are free of stereotypes and they show sensitivity to particular groups of people. Artwork depicts a variety of ages and a variety of skin tones. In transforming congregations, there is a balance of men and women, youth and children who participate in up-front leadership. The hymns and readings use a wide assortment of feminine, masculine and gender-neutral images when referring to God, and men and women hear themselves addressed in scripture.

Transforming congregations do everything they can to make their facilities accessible to all people. They install ramps and remove pews so that those in wheelchairs can navigate various levels in the building and can sit with others in worship. They widen hallways and restroom stalls and provide handicap parking spaces next to the door. They offer large print hymnals and bulletins for those with visual impairments or project the words to the songs on a screen. They provide amplified listening devices for the hard-of-hearing.

Understanding that children also have special needs, transforming congregations take intentional steps to include young ones in worship. Since children have a hard time sitting still and being quiet for large periods of time, they provide space in the sanctuary where babies can crawl and children can wiggle under the watchful eye of an adult. A mat on the floor or smaller chairs around a children's table make things more comfortable. Incorporating motions to songs or prayers keeps children involved.

Transforming congregations teach young ones that there are times for singing, times for praying, times for listening, and times for creating in worship. They help children memorize the sung and spoken parts of the liturgy which remain the same from week to week so the young ones more easily can participate in worship. They teach a posture that children can assume when it is time for corporate prayer. They provide art materials for children to use during the sermon or homily, and often display that art on bulletin boards, on the front of worship bulletins, or on the screen in the worship space. Transforming congregations do not put children on display, but they include them as readers and musicians in worship and often invite them to offer petitions during the prayers of the people.

Transforming congregations look for ways to include the gifts of each person in appropriate ways in the life of the church. "Who knew that a French horn would be such a great addition to our music group that leads singing in worship?" one young woman exclaimed as she reflected back on the way the church had integrated the talents of a newcomer. "We found out two men who were new to our congregation worked in a restaurant. They were delighted when we asked them to help with the mid-week meal," another woman said.

When transforming congregations practice the spiritual habit of including, people come to know themselves as beloved children of God with gifts to share. But that does not mean newcomers should be given positions of leadership right away. Many a church has gotten itself in trouble by giving immature or unhealthy people positions of authority before the church came to know those people well! It is important to welcome those bearing particular gifts by finding places where those gifts can best be used to serve the vision, mission, and values established by the whole church.

Boundaries are needed to create trustworthy space. Transforming congregations establish clear behavioral expectations and maintain an unwavering vigilance to make sure those boundaries are maintained by everyone. At a minimum, the behavioral expectations assure the physical and psychological safety of everyone. Practices such as asking those who work with children and youth to complete background checks, making sure there are always two people in a classroom or a car with children or youth, and developing a check-in system for the nursery protect both young and old from sexual misconduct, physical or emotional abuse, or harassment. At their best, those boundaries guarantee the spiritual safety so young people can develop strong egos and then develop the courage to relinquish those egos to become spiritually mature adults.

Some transforming congregations list boundaries that create spiritual safety in the form of a congregational covenant.[97] That covenant might name expectations such as

- **We speak out of our own experience** rather than out of our own beliefs.[98]
- **We take responsibility** for our own actions.
- **We listen and learn** from one another.

- **We respect differences.**
- **We don't try to "fix"** one another.
- **We are not afraid** to ask questions or to share our doubts.
- **We abide by the decisions made** by our governing body, whether those decisions reflect our own views or not.

The covenant guides the life of small groups and classes. It governs the dialogue that takes place when the church gathers to deliberate before making a decision.

Yet as important as it is to establish such behavioral boundaries, transforming congregations understand it is even more important for participants to hold each other accountable for adhering to the covenant they create. If violations of the behavioral expectations are ignored, people are likely to drift away. When violations are addressed directly and privately, people learn to trust that the congregation is a safe place where they can grow into their God-given potential. (See Appendix I to write a behavioral covenant.)

In transforming congregations, a behavioral covenant and safe church practices are the established norm for the congregation. Congregational leaders work together to make sure that norm is upheld. To do that, they put the common good above the possibility of hurting an individual's feelings. They call out those who violate the congregational covenant in a caring, unwavering manner in order to create trustworthy community for all.

QUESTIONS FOR REFLECTION

1. When have you experienced true hospitality for the soul? What were the components present in that situation which made you feel welcomed?

2. What are the subtle ways we judge others? How can we eliminate judgment from our lives?

3. What practices could you put in place to make your congregation safer?

4. What boundaries would you like to see listed in a covenant for your congregation?

SPIRITUAL HABIT 8
QUESTIONING

There is a profound and painful disconnect between what
Christianity has become and what we perceive it should be.[99]
— Diana Butler Bass

Transmitting tradition has always been one task of religion. Tradition made up of a narrative which sets forth a particular view of reality, a set of values that have stood the test of time, and an effective strategy for living gives religion its authenticity. As each new generation enters into a religious tradition, it steps into a story that was told long before it arrived and that will continue long after it is gone. Newcomers initiated into a religion learn truth that transcends historical circumstance. They engage in practices they did not invent which root them in something larger than themselves.

To the extent that a tradition connects its followers to the presence of the sacred, it continues to be a living source of meaning, guidance, and power. However, religion can become distorted over time, losing its ability to address the deep longings of the soul. It can become too narrow, focusing on one aspect of the tradition while ignoring other facets. It can become corrupt, exploiting the tradition for personal gain. It can become stale, draining the tradition of its ability to speak a relevant word of wisdom.

This is a time when the Christian tradition has lost credibility with the American public. Researcher and historian, Diana Butler Bass suggests that several events which took place at the beginning of the 21st Century have fueled the current discontent:

1. News commentators blamed religion for the terrorist attacks on September 11, 2001
2. It came to light that since the 1960s, the Roman Catholic church had systematically covered up cases of sexual abuse by priests.

3. After the Episcopal Diocese of New Hampshire elected openly gay priest, V. Gene Robinson as bishop, the public watched nasty fighting between church members on the right and on the left, as they made homosexuality the dominant moral issue of the day.

4. The religious right put forth a mix of faith and politics that was at odds with the cultural and spiritual values of younger Americans and became the public face of Christianity in the United States.

5. The national economic crisis in 2007 weakened religious institutions.[100]

As a result of these and other factors, when younger people are asked what they think about Christianity today, they say

1. The church is irrelevant.
2. The church has become too narrow in its beliefs.
3. Christians are judgmental, mean and critical.
4. Individuals within the church are not committed to spiritual growth.[101]

Like a house that has shifted on its foundation, transforming congregations recognize that the Christian tradition must be trued up if it is to regain its integrity, especially in the eyes of younger adults.

THE SUBVERSION OF THE HISTORIC PROTESTANT CHURCH

The segment of the population which claims no religious affiliation is growing faster today than any Protestant, Catholic, or Evangelical strand of the church.[102]

Yet unlike the increasing number of people in Europe who no longer believe in God, the churchless population in the United States is not primarily secular in nature. Most people who are not affiliated with a congregation do not reject God even if they reject the institutions and theological teachings that have been bearers of religion in the past. They value intellectual freedom. They seek personal growth and personal peace. They concern themselves with the large questions of how human life fits into the overall scheme of things. They care about issues such as simple living, human rights, justice for the poor, peace, and care for the earth and they want to find ways to live with courage and compassion in the world.[103]

If that demographic group had been living in the first part of the 20th Century, those people probably could have found a home in the historic Protestant "brand name" denominations that served as the primary face of Christianity at that time. Although those denominations varied as to style of worship and particularity of practice, they all reflected similar values which allowed them to work together ecumenically:

- **Faith and reason** which approached religion with both the heart and the mind
- **Religious tolerance** that protected the rights of each individual to worship without fear in the manner they chose
- **Reliance on God's grace** that did not depend on human striving
- **A scholarly approach to Biblical interpretation** that considered context, authorship, and audience of each passage
- **The priesthood of all believers** that expected lay people to study, lead, and think theologically alongside clergy
- **Discipleship** that meant following Christ into the world to heal the great social sins of exploitation, injustice, and inhumanity that were present in the workplace, in the political arena and in the social conditions of the day

However, in the second half of the 20th Century, other forms became the most well-known expressions of the Christian tradition. One form, discussed earlier, was Golden Rule Christianity. It has become essentially obsolete in the landscape of the 21st Century. Yet, there were two other theological expressions of Christianity that took center stage during that time which deserve mention. In many places, one or both of them have become what come to mind when most people hear the word "Christian." They are the theology of fundamentalism and the theology of prosperity.

When Fundamentalism first came on the scene in the 1920s, it took up residence in the holiness Free Church traditions which were more Pentecostal in nature; but gradually, as population shifts took place, it found its way into historic Protestant denominations as well.[104] Now theological thought is no longer divided along denominational lines; one is as likely to find variations on Fundamentalist beliefs in a church with a Methodist, Presbyterian, or Lutheran logo out front as within an Assembly of God or a Foursquare congregation.

When Fundamentalism first came on the scene, Gresham Machen was its mouthpiece. He countered the public voice of historical Protestant denominations with five fundamentals. Fundamentalism claimed that the Virgin Birth of Christ was proof of Christ's divinity. It asserted that Jesus rose bodily from the grave and that Christ would imminently come again in glory to judge the world. Where the historic Protestant church made room for several interpretations of the meaning of Christ's death and resurrection,[105] Fundamentalists insisted the satisfaction theory of redemption put forth by Anselm of Canterbury in the 11th Century was the only correct view. That doctrine asserted that Christ obediently took his place on the cross, dying as a substitution for humanity to appease a vengeful God who required an atoning blood sacrifice in order to pardon those born in sin.

Rather than looking at the Bible as a book of many voices, Machen claimed the Bible constituted one voice—the voice of God—that spoke without error. Rather than taking into account the historical context within which the various books of the Bible were written, he asserted that the Bible was an a-contextual book for all times and all places. A-contextual meant a verse from any Biblical book could be lifted out to serve as an authority in the modern age, not only in matters of faith, but in matters of morality, history, and science.

Two millennia of Christian theology had made use of the rich language of metaphor and symbol, but Fundamentalists subscribed to the notion that the only true faith was a literal faith. The historic Protestant tradition emphasized the building of God's kingdom on earth as it is in heaven, but Fundamentalists stressed the judgment of God and the demise of the world as we know it.[106]

The other theology that characterizes the face of Christianity in some places is the Prosperity Gospel. Prosperity theology was born out of healing revivals conducted by charismatics such as Oral Roberts in the 1950s. It claimed God wanted all humans to have the gifts of good physical health and economic prosperity. To receive those gifts, people only had to have enough faith. In the 1960s and 1970s, prosperity theology was taught by televangelists and eventually it found a home in non-denominational charismatic multi-site mega-churches such as The Potter's House.[107]

Some congregations not only preached the message of entitlement in the United States, they exported that message to other nations through their missionary efforts. Through new church plants overseas, they taught young people in developing countries that God desired for them a life of wealth and privilege filled with the latest North American fashions, the best cars, and the fanciest homes. Those young people focused so much on gaining their own personal success they became numb to the poverty and political oppression of their neighbors.

When *The Prayer of Jabez* hit the New York Times Best-Seller List in 2000, prosperity theology found its way into historic Protestant denominations.[108] Book groups learned how to ask God to bless them, to increase what they owned, and to keep them from hurt and harm.[109] Later in that decade, members started reading Joel Osteen who further popularized prosperity theology.[110]

CRISIS OF LEGITIMACY

Many people today reject the Christian tradition because they reject the theologies presented by the public face of Christianity today. Those who left the historic Protestant church in recent decades say they did so because their congregation became too narrow in its beliefs.[111] In today's world of evolving complexity, globalization, and racial and religious pluralism, they found it impossible to believe that any one religion had a monopoly on the truth. They had friends of many different races who found wisdom in other world

religions. They saw validity in spiritual paths other than Christianity. It did not make sense to them that a God who so loved the
world would limit salvation only to those who confessed faith in
Jesus Christ. In addition, those who believed gay, lesbian, bi-sexual
and transgender people should enjoy the same rights as other North
Americans found it difficult to be part of a church community that
referred to homosexuality as an abomination to God.

Twenty-nine percent of those who are no longer affiliated with
the historic Protestant church say they quit attending worship services because their church began interpreting the Bible too literally.
Where once it taught them to consider the time, place, and audience for which a passage was written, to pay attention to the kind
of literature it represented, and to view the Bible as a conversation
among many perspectives, their congregation started regarding all
verses as readily applicable for today's context. It started teaching
that scripture was one monolithic message without error, written
by God, which contained no cultural bias or contradiction. At that
point, those who could not view all verses in scripture as equally
authoritative quit going to church altogether.

Others say they left the church because they could not believe
humans are born in sin nor were they interested in committing
themselves to a religion based in the fear of eternal punishment.
For them, salvation was less about rescuing people for heaven than
helping people find wholeness in the here and now, especially in
light of the growing gap between rich and the poor and the deple-
tion of renewable planetary resources. They cared about peace and
were not interested in worshiping a vengeful God who required a
blood sacrifice. In fact, the doctrine of substitutionary atonement
seemed absurd to them. They grew weary of the church asking them
to choose between their intellectual integrity and their faith. Rather
than live a hypocritical life, believing one thing and belonging to a
church that believed another, they chose to leave organized religion
behind.

Yet others left because the church's promise of success did not
materialize. Like the majority of Americans, they found that the
happiness they pursued continued to elude them. Even though

they lived a world where per-capita income was on the rise, life expectancy was increasing, violence was decreasing, and the level of education was higher than ever before, unremitting bad feelings with no specific cause plagued them like a low grade fever.[112]

Adjusting for population growth, ten times as many citizens of the United States experience "uni-polar depression" than people did half a century ago.[113] Pursuing more wealth has left many people feeling exhausted, fragmented and lonely. Pursuing self-interests has not brought about contentment. Acquiring more stuff has not provided the comfort they had hoped for. Filling up time with busyness has not offered meaning or purpose. No matter how much they buy, how much power they gain, how many interests they pursue, many Americans still have the nagging sense that they do not have enough, that they are not enough, that there is always something more that they cannot quite reach beyond an ever receding horizon.

THE SPIRITUAL PRACTICE OF QUESTIONING

Even though this is an age when people care more about what the church does than what it believes, transforming congregations know they must lessen the gap between people's experience of God and the church's teaching about God if the church is once again to become a reliable source of wisdom. Beliefs matter. Transforming congregations that are creedal churches help individuals discover a deeper truth in the words they recite; those that are non-creedal churches create safe space where individuals can work out their own guiding beliefs. They create space within their own tradition where people have the freedom to honestly express doubts, to say what they do not believe, to ask questions that don't have predetermined answers, and to wonder about the mysteries of the universe.

Around tables in church basements, in coffee shops and bars, and in the public square, transforming congregations engage in robust theological dialogue that invites people to wrestle with complex issues, ethical dilemmas, and strategies for living that make sense in today's world. The purpose of the dialogue is not to create a new creed; it is to reconcile what divides people from themselves, from God, from neighbor, and from the earth.

One transforming congregation holds theological dialogue in the community pub on Tuesday nights. Participants from the church and interested parties who live in the neighborhood gather for an hour-long guided conversation. Not all the members of the group call themselves Christian. Some identify as secular humanists, others feel most at home in the Sufi tradition. Yet all of them come together to explore the deep issues of life. They are not there to convert each other to a particular point of view but to listen with respect to each other's truths, trusting each person to take away what he or she needs from the evening.

Another transforming congregation hosts a theological forum on Sunday morning. Each session begins with an open-ended question posed by a video resource. Participants share out of their own experiences and viewpoints. Other historical and contemporary theologians are brought into the mix. An interplay results between the inherited tradition and people's own knowing, between the past and the present, and between what has been and what will be.

Transforming congregations do not try to stop change or even to slow it down. Instead, they think theologically about the new questions that change creates Here are but a few examples of the kind of inquiries they are making:

- What do biology, astronomy, and physics reveal about God?
- What does it mean to follow Jesus in a multi-religious world?
- What new ways of knowing can humans develop to connect with the power and the presence of the Spirit that lives within and among them?
- What moral responsibility do human beings carry for the welfare of the planet?
- How do Christians discern with those of other faiths or no faith at all which wise actions to take for the common good?

- How do Christians practice peace and also stand against systemic sins of greed, racism, corruption, patriarchy, and violence?

Like the householder who "brings out of his treasure what is new and what is old,"[114] transforming congregations sort through the Christian tradition they have inherited to see which theological understandings they will carry into the future, which they will discard, and which they will continue to true up for a new day.

QUESTIONS FOR REFLECTION

1. What kind of theology is expressed through the sermons, teaching, and hymnody of your congregation?

2. Which theological understandings are hard for you to believe?

3. What barriers must the church overcome in order to reconnect with the growing churchless population?

4. How could your congregation create safe space for theological inquiry and conversation?

SPIRITUAL HABIT 9
BUILDING CAPACITY

We have a language of intimacy that is now based upon wounds.[115]
— Caroline Myss

The Gospel of John tells the story of a man who was ill for thirty-eight years. Each day, the man sat in a portico by the pool of Bethzatha with all the other invalids who were blind or lame or paralyzed. It was said that when the surface of the water was stirred, the first person into the pool would be healed of his or her infirmity. One day Jesus walked by and stopped to speak to the man. "Do you want to be made well?" Jesus asked him. "Sir, I have no one to put me into the pool when the water is stirred up; and while I am making my way, someone else steps down ahead of me." But Jesus took away all his excuses. "Stand up, take your mat, and walk," Jesus said to the man. At once the man was made well, and he took up his mat and began to walk.[116]

There is no way to know for sure what was going through the man's mind before he met Jesus, but it is possible to observe his words and his behavior: He lay by the pool every day for thirty-eight years. He refused to take responsibility for himself. He blamed others for his inability to get ahead in life. He described himself as a victim of life's circumstances. He depended on others to meet his needs. He kept doing the same thing day after day even though that course of action did not make things better.

So Jesus' question, "Do you want to be made well?" was exactly the right one. Healing would not only change the man's body, it would change his image of himself and the relationship he had established with his co-dependent friends. Did he really want something different?

Some congregations create a culture of victimization. They organize themselves around the needs of those who have been wounded by the circumstances of their lives and who use those wounds as an excuse for never moving on. In my college years, I belonged to a church group that used wounds as a means of establishing intimacy with one another. Through the honesty of personal sharing, we bared our souls. Tears were shed, anger was expressed, and masks were removed. In that group, we learned who we were apart from the roles we played. But we also learned some other lessons that did not serve us as well: we figured out that dramatic emotional sharing was the way to get close to others and we concluded that playing the victim was the way to be heard.

One congregation that I will call "Good Shepherd Church" organizes its life around personal wounds. The pastor often gets phone calls from church participants who believe they have been wronged, ignored, or unrecognized and he gives them his undivided attention. Individuals within the church often react to change with highly charged emotions and little dramas often play themselves out among members of the congregation. The leaders of the church cater to those who complain the most. When people break boundaries, those leaders let the infraction go because they do not want to stir up more trouble.

Good Shepherd takes pride in its caring ministries; yet it has trouble moving beyond a focus on its members to a focus on its mission. Whenever it comes to a point of decision, the congregation finds it difficult to agree on what to do next. When the church actually votes on a course of action, the minority who does not support the choice made by the majority find a way to subvert it. The congregation often finds itself in stalemate because the leaders choose not to implement agreed-upon actions in order to appease those who disagree.

Researcher and healer Carolyn Myss suggests that congregations such as Good Shepherd function out of an unspoken pact that contains the following agreements:[117]

1. We will be there to support each other through any difficult memories associated with the wounds we have experienced.
2. That support will include reorganizing our life and ministry around the needs of our wounded participants.

3. If required, we will carry out the responsibilities of those who are wounded, showing how sincere we are in their support.

4. We will always encourage our wounded partners to talk as much as they need to about their wounds and to take as much time as necessary for recovery,

5. We will accept, with minimal friction, all weaknesses and shortcomings rooted in wounds, since acceptance is crucial to healing.

That pact looks like caring—the kind of ministry that a compassionate congregation which follows Jesus would practice. But, in fact, the way Jesus cared for people was much different from the way Good Shepherd Church carries out its pastoral ministry.

THE SPIRITUAL HABIT OF CAPACITY-BUILDING

In the story about the man by the pool, Jesus showed love, not by sympathizing with his plight, but by challenging him in a no-nonsense way. "Stand up, take your mat, and walk," Jesus said. Instead of supporting the man's identity as victim, Jesus gave him a new identity as a man who had been made well. He built up the man's inner capacity so he could take responsibility for his own life. Instead of lying by the pool day after day, the man finally chose a different course of action: he took up his mat and began to walk on his own two feet.

North American missionaries sent overseas always build into their work a capacity-building component that challenges their neighbors to increase their ability to care for themselves and their families. At *Mision Cristiana* in Nicaragua, capacity-building involves distributing seed packets so families can grow their own food, produce a crop they can sell, and provide seed for even more families. In Mozambique, it involves taking applications for micro-loans from women who want to start their own business and expecting them to give back some of their profits so even more women can receive such loans.

Capacity-building not only asks "what" is wrong, it asks "why" it is wrong and who benefits from maintaining the status quo. It tries to get beneath symptoms to address causes. As transforming congregations get involved in capacity-building, they often find themselves engaged in political advocacy in addition to service. They feed, clothe, and house people, but they also work to dismantle systems that keep people from accessing the resources they need to feed, clothe and house themselves.

Capacity-building invests in people, not just programs. It treats individuals as subjects rather than as objects of charity. It involves education, skill-building, and economic assistance which empowers people rather than creating further dependency. It encourages those who receive a hand up to extend their hand to others who need that same kind of opportunity. It calls them to take responsibility for their own well-being.

In one small transforming congregation in Washington State, capacity-building took hold as the church shifted its focus away from mission to those without homes, to mission with those without homes. It happened as the church began noticing that the same people kept showing up at their soup kitchen week after week. "Nothing is changing in these people's lives," they said to each other. "We need to do something different." After months of prayer and discernment, they began to see that addictions seemed to be at the root of many of their neighbors' inability to keep a roof over their head or to work. They began imagining a recovery ministry in which everyone would be encouraged to live prayerfully, to show respect, to practice compassion, and to contribute to the community.

Accountability seemed to be the missing piece. They were handing out food each week, but not expecting much from those they were serving. This new awareness caused them to change how they were doing things. Because most of their neighbors had never belonged to anything, they created a "members only" club. Those who wanted to receive the benefits of the club such as hot meals, connections to counseling services, housing resources, classes in life skills, and relapse prevention were asked to attend a circle of accountability each week and to contribute in some way to the life of the community. After the meal, one person was expected to wipe down tables, another to clean the restrooms, and another to wash dishes. Capacity-building asks people to give, not just to take. In so doing, it treats each individual as somebody with something to offer for the sake of the common good.

HEALTH IN THE BODY

The New Testament spoke about the church as a living system—the Body of Christ. The body consisted of many members all carrying out their individual functions; but it was more than just the sum of its parts. It was an integrated organism that suffered together when one member suffered and rejoiced together when one member was honored.[118] It was an interdependent being which was affected by the dynamic relationships between and among the various parts. For the body to be healthy it was important for individual members to do their jobs, but it was also important for the body to function as one unified whole. Too much separateness and the body lost its sense of connection; too much sameness and the body lost the distinctive character of its parts. There had to be a balance between individuality and conformity for the body to remain healthy.

Sickness threatens the integrity of the human body; anxiety-producing change threatens the integrity of the Body of Christ. When a congregation experiences money problems, conflict over the style of worship, harm to property or to a participant, the church can lose its balance, opting for each person to go his or her own way without regard for others or expecting everyone to act in unison without regard for individual uniqueness.

Systems analysts such as Peter Steinke, Edwin Friedman, and Murray Bowen believe that when a congregation is stressed by change, there is a tendency to move from direct one-on-one communication to triangled communication which involves a third party.[119] Individuals stop talking to each other and start talking about each other. People mount campaigns over the telephone or email each other to garner support for their opinions. Meetings become shouting matches. Some people bully meeker members of the congregation, threatening to leave if things do not go their way.

When conflict erupts in a congregation, the system becomes less resilient and less imaginative. Conflict magnifies differences between people or groups, it heightens secrecy, and it demands immediate relief from the stress of the moment. When stressed by change, congregational members tend to become rigid in their protection of the church building or in their control of the church's finances. They often begin micro-managing every project, watching every penny, and scrutinizing every ministry initiative.

HEALTHY LEADERSHIP

Before leaders can help a church manage conflict, they must be able to manage their own reactivity by acting calmly and courageously even when stressed. Before they can deal with anxiety in the Body of Christ, they must first learn to regulate anxiety in their own bodies through self-reflection and prayer. Before they can promote health in the church they must learn to express themselves with integrity rather than looking to others' expectations to define how they should think or act. It takes practice and commitment to hold a steady course when the ship is listing.

But when leaders can learn to control their own reactions, they can be invaluable in helping to lessen anxiety and conflict in the church. When they stay spiritually grounded, they can help a congregation regain its balance. When they continually define who they are and what they stand for, they can re-focus attention on the church's vision, mission, and values. When they stay in place rather than cutting and running when things get tough, they can nurture transformation long enough so it actually may take root.

When asked how she helped the congregation to become a multi-generational church, one pastor said, "I learned not to take complaints personally. I couldn't be a 'nice' pastor and get the work done; I had to constantly set boundaries for people who would not set them for themselves. Eventually other church leaders learned to do that too. Twenty-five years ago, they were trying to keep everyone happy. They did not want to lose people or their contributions to the church. Then they started standing up to church participants who were undermining the church's progress with their constant complaining. Just a few people doing things differently changed the system."

When anxiety showed itself in that congregation, the leaders stepped up to hold each other accountable and to make sure boundaries were maintained so the church could be a safe place for all. Sometimes that meant calling out judgmental or intimidating behavior, even if confronting those behaviors resulted in some people leaving the church. Leaders also fostered health during times of stress by helping the church focus on its purpose rather than on its preferences. They created the expectation that all congregational participants would adhere to the church's policies and covenants. When congregational participants looked for simple, quick fixes, when they threatened or manipulated, when they garnered support for their own position, when they sabotaged plans or placed blame or criticized, the leaders steadily and persistently called the church back to the decisions it had made as a whole.

Leaders in transforming congregations do not give much time or attention to emotionally immature individuals who are easily hurt or slow to heal from perceived wrongs. They do not try to appease those people by giving them a larger role in the decision-making processes of the congregation. They do not allow one person or a group of individuals to bully the rest of the congregation.

Leaders in transforming congregations teach people how to forgive. They know that holding on to wounds siphons off precious life-energy, so they help people learn how to offer forgiveness to those who have wounded them in the past so they can live more fully in the present. One pastor put it this way: "It became clear to me that we just were not going to be able to move on as a church until we released the resentments from the past that were binding us up and keeping us stuck." That transforming congregation held a service of reconciliation where congregational participants offered and received the forgiveness that freed up their energy for new ministry.

To forgive does not require someone to forget. It does not require an apology from the person who has caused the pain, nor does it require that person to be present in the same room. It only requires the person who has been wronged to let go of the bitterness they may have been holding onto and to allow their wounds to heal. Forgiveness fosters health and well-being in the church community. It allows individuals to quit playing the victim, to stop blaming others for the circumstances in which they find themselves, and to take responsibility for the ways their own actions have contributed to those circumstances.

Forgiveness frees people so they can stand up and walk. It builds capacity that does not tolerate whining or excuses, lone-ranger behavior, or coercion. Instead it offers tough love that challenges each person to choose the path that leads to wholeness, even in the midst of difficult circumstances. It helps connect people with the resources they need to in order to grow in their ability to care for themselves. Like Jesus' ministry, it opens the eyes of the blind, proclaims good news to the poor, and liberates the captives so they can determine the course of their own lives.

QUESTIONS FOR REFLECTION

1. How does your congregation organize its life and ministry around wounds? How does it organize its life and ministry around health?

2. Are there factors which keep your congregation from following through on decisions which are made by the church as a whole? What would need to happen to allow you to implement the commitments you have made together?

3. What wounds does your congregation need to release in order to live in freedom? Who do you need to forgive in order to let go of past hurts?

4. How could you make capacity-building a bigger part of your congregation's missional efforts?

Connecting with the World

SPIRITUAL HABIT 10
GIVING THANKS

Geese appear high over us,
pass, and the sky closes. Abandon,
as in love or sleep, holds
them to their way, clear
in the ancient faith: what we need is here.[120]
— Wendell Berry

At the end of the *Chronicles of Narnia*, C.S. Lewis describes a feast of abundance laid out in front of a gathering of dwarfs.[121] The table is set beneath a grove of trees reaching up to a beautiful blue sky and flowers are all around. On the table are meat pies, trifles, ices, and goblets of good wine. But the dwarfs cannot perceive any of it. They huddle together in a little circle facing one another and complain about the pitch blackness and smell of manure in the poky little hole of a stable in which they believe they are sitting. As they grab and snatch at the food, they grumble about moldy turnips and decaying cabbage leaves they are eating. As they quarrel with each other, they gripe about the putrid water they've been given to drink. Why can't they recognize the good gifts that are before them? Lewis tells us their minds have become their prisons. They have become cynical; even with abundance all around, they see only scarcity.

Scarcity is a closed system, a zero-sum proposition. When we live in scarcity, we feel the need to protect the little we have because it may be all we ever get. Scarcity makes us critical of others' actions and prone to instant indignation. It is hard to be generous when we believe we do not have enough. "Better to take care of our own first," we think, "after all, if we share what we have with others, what will happen to us if there is some unforeseen emergency?

Doesn't charity begin at home?" Scarcity makes us calculating, stingy, and cynical.

When we are cynical, the future appears to be more of the present, only worse. There is no room for surprise, for the unexpected turn of events. Cynicism is a pinched, tight state of mind that steals away joy. It causes us to focus on the negative until we no longer see the good. When we live in cynicism, we quit believing in possibility; we squelch new ideas before they really have a hearing. Cynicism causes us to be overly serious, overly sensitive. When we live in cynicism, we become complaining curmudgeons who blame others for adding to our misery. When we live in cynicism, life becomes just one never-ending list of chores that need to be done with not enough time to do them. Over time, cynicism produces a kind of soul weariness that can cause us to quit caring. Dorothy Sayers observes that weariness, "believes nothing, cares to know nothing, seeks to know nothing, loves nothing, hates nothing, finds purpose in nothing and remains alive because there is nothing for which it will die."[122] When we live in cynicism, we lose our focus, our courage, and our hope.

The Gospels all tell a story about a time when Jesus' disciples saw only scarcity. "Come away to a deserted place and rest awhile," Jesus said to them. He recognized they had not had enough time even to eat. Of course, when they got off by themselves, the disciples discovered the crowds had followed. That meant they had another problem: not enough food to go around. "Send the people away, Jesus," they said, "so they can go to the surrounding country and villages and buy something to eat." But Jesus told the disciples, "You give them something to eat." Dumbfounded, the disciples asked, "Are we to go and buy bread for all these people?" Cynicism had crept in; they were sure they did not have enough power to accomplish such a monumental task.

Jesus' disciples perceived only insufficiency--a shortage of time, a shortage of resources, and a shortage of power. In that situation, the disciples just wanted to throw up their hands, to give up. They could see no way forward, no way to accomplish what seemed like an impossible task. But Jesus saw another way.

He asked the disciples, "How many loaves have you?" Then, he sent them off to inventory the resources they had in their possession: five loaves and two fish. Jesus told his disciples to get the people organized. Jesus then took the five loaves and two fish, gave thanks for them, broke, and shared them. All the people ate, all were filled, and there were even leftovers! Scarcity turned into plenty.

Transforming congregations report that they too experience plenty when they begin to act as if they have enough time to do what is important, as if there is enough giftedness to accomplish the task, as if there is enough energy available to them through the restoring power of God. When they take time for being instead of just for doing, the time they do have seems to expand. When they take inventory of what they possess and give it over to God's purposes, resources seem to multiply. When they recognize the providence of God, they begin to see more and more good gifts all around

DOING MORE WITH LESS

Currently most North American adults spend at least eight hours a day staring at some kind of screen,[123] yet they crave even more. Worried that they might miss out on something, they find it difficult to look away. Research shows that, in many cases, technology is not providing more freedom as much as it is creating an addiction-like dependence that steals time when it seems like there already are not enough hours in the day.

The United States is a nation of workaholics. In order to make ends meet, workers put in more hours on the job than those in any other industrialized nation.[124] They juggle their own hectic schedules along with their children's classes, games, and performances. In fact, American families have so much going on, many cannot seem to find time to have dinner together. It is easier to pick up fast food or microwave meals individuals can make for themselves whenever they get home.

The American consumer culture begins with the notion that time is scarce. Transforming congregations begin with the idea that they have enough time to do what is essential and they teach people how to make choices about using the time they have. In a counter-cultural move, they subvert the idea that people must always be busy, always going, always doing by inviting individuals to choose some time each day for *being* each day.

Just as transforming congregations encourage individuals to prioritize their time, the church body itself begins to sort out what is truly important for them to do as a spiritual community. Instead of maintaining the same calendar of church events year after year, they let go of those occasions and projects that have become nothing more than church chores. Instead of continuing to practice certain rituals, they ask the reason behind the rituals. If traditions no longer make sense, they quit doing them. Instead of trying to fill every church leadership position, they ask which positions are indispensable and they eliminate the rest, streamlining the church structure.

"We used to get so tired," one young woman told me. "At nomination time, we never had enough names to fill the slots. Then we reduced the number of elected positions we had. Now I think we're actually spending more time doing the work of the church, but it is no longer busy work. We're not all burned out like we used to be." Her comments are typical of what I have heard in many transforming congregations that believe time spent doing ministry that matters can be energizing.

When transforming congregations feel like there is not enough time, they discipline themselves to slow down instead of speeding up. They counter the drive to fill every minute of every day by honoring the Sabbath and taking time to connect with the power of the Spirit. Some transforming congregations declare whole months or even whole years "Sabbath time" when they intentionally take a break from church programming in order to rest and to consider the next steps the Spirit calls them to take. Some invite leaders to take a "Sabbath year" when they do no work for the church. Some congregations suspend a part of the by-laws for a time in order to try out a new way of structuring themselves. Transforming congregations know that the time spent dreaming, planning,

building relationships, and listening for the v
time wasted.

FUNDING THE MISSION

As transforming congregations grow their m͏.   ⸗ɟ also look for new ways to expand the funding for tha͏. ͏mission. They take seriously the predictions of church development officers who say proportional giving has already become a thing of the past. In the 21st Century, fewer people want to give to a general fund for the maintenance of an organization; they want to give to ministries that are making a visible difference in the lives of people. That means that if the church wants to finance its mission, it will first have to make a case for the effectiveness of its ministry.

Even transforming congregations who still underwrite most of their budget through an annual pledge drive learn to depend less on the kind of unified giving familiar to past generations. They rely more on directed giving which is the preferred mode of philanthropy of younger people. They work hard at telling the story both inside and outside the church of how their congregation is engaged in transforming the world. They put together narrative budgets, brochures, and presentations. They make provision for congregational participants to fund those ministries they care about. They put up posters, take out ads, and create websites that let people beyond the congregation know what the church is doing and how it is making an impact.

But transforming congregations do not just rely on directed giving; they look to a variety of income streams to support their ministries. Some are fortunate enough to have funds invested by their ancestors in the faith which provide interest each year to support the work of the church. Some collect rent from organizations or other churches that use their buildings or parking lots. Some congregations have taken to writing grants to support their mission. Some look to other organizations to acquire grants for programs that overlap with ministries of the church. Some establish separate non-profit businesses to support the church's mission.

One small congregation runs a coffee house that showcases the paintings of local artists and the original compositions of local musicians. It has become a community center for the town where it is located. Church participants take turns serving as baristas and baking pastries to sell with the coffee. The business is a corporation that is licensed as separate from the church; but the proceeds from the business fund the congregation's ministries.

Transforming congregations create opportunities for people both inside and outside the church to give. Some hold fundraisers such as dinners, rummage sales, bazaars, or evenings of entertainment and invite their neighbors to come. Some post stories on the web and provide opportunities for people to give on-line. Some invite merchants to support ministries with donated goods and services.

As part of their spiritual habit of gratitude, transforming congregations frequently make opportunities to thank people for all the ways they give. They write notes, make phone calls, take donors to lunch, and list their partners' names in publications. They give thanks for the resources they have and for the people who make their ministries possible.

ASSET INVENTORY

When congregations focus on what is missing from their lives: they will tell you that they do not have enough people, money, or energy to carry out their ministries. Contrast that with congregations that focus on what they have. They regularly take inventory of the assets they possess that can help them move forward in ministry.

Some begin with inventories that help individuals within the congregation determine their own gifts. Those results help people better discern their vocational calling. In transforming congregations many individuals tell personal stories which seem to all begin with the line "A few years ago, I never would have dreamed I'd be doing...." One man discovered a heart for leading Bible study with prison inmates. Another man found a way to use his carpentry skills to build Habitat houses on Saturday. One woman enrolled in an on-line seminary. Another woman found she had the gift of presence and now she serves by sitting down with a senior citizen once a week just to listen to what that person has to say.

Transforming congregations also take note of the resources they hold as a church community. Do they have a building? How many of its rooms could be used to house the homeless or feed the hungry? Would any of them be a good fit for a non-profit group? How could they extend the use of their sanctuary or their musical instruments beyond worship times? How could their kitchen function better? Do they have showers in their restrooms? If so, could those be used more fully in the service of their neighbors? Transforming congregations try to put every aspect of their space into the service of their mission.

Transforming congregations also recognize the leadership in their midst as a resource. They pay attention to the particular skills, talents, and passions of both clergy and lay leaders (and help the church see where they need to recruit other partners or hire other staff to help them fill any gaps). They encourage their leaders to work out of their sense of call from God and not out of a sense of obligation. They allow their leaders to lead without putting roadblocks in their way, and they make room for those leaders to mentor, equip, and motivate others to use their gifts as well.

In addition to quantifiable factors, transforming congregations identify the more intangible qualities that have been a source of life and energy throughout their history. They pay attention to the spiritual gifts that have been present since the founding of the congregation. For example, while considering its character, one congregation noted how much it had enjoyed singing. That conversation became the impetus to start a new community choir involving neighborhood youth. One congregation observed how they had always taken risks, even purchasing a new lot for parking cars back in 1929 when everyone else was stashing their money away in their mattresses. That insight helped them gather the courage to take another bold step even though they did not have a lot of money in the bank: buying computers for youth to use in a much-needed after-school ministry.

For transforming congregations, relationships are themselves intangible assets to be recognized. The connections church participants make with each other and their neighbors activate the imagination and release potential energy in ways that are not possible when one person or one group controls the life and ministry of the church. By nurturing those relationships, insights emerge, coalitions take shape, new ideas come to light, and creativity is enlarged.

Transforming congregations seek assets in the neighborhood where they are located. If other non-profit businesses have grant writers with a proven track record, transforming congregations may choose to partner with them to enhance the church's ministries. For example, one congregation in California gave over several rooms for an organization to use for transitional housing. In return, the non-profit used grant money to bring the church building's wiring and plumbing up to code, to remodel the restrooms, to furnish a new meeting room, and to create a new set of offices to serve as the organization's workspace.

Other transforming congregations find partners in the community who are working toward goals that complement their ministry. One pastor of a transforming congregation told me, "There are those in our town who would never give a dime to keep the gears of the church cranking away, but they will give to the ministries we're doing now, because they can see those ministries are making a difference in people's lives." Transforming congregations often augment the financial gifts of their own members with fundraisers that bring in the gifts of others in the neighborhood.

Similarly, those congregations also find gifts of time and talent in their city or town. One congregation forged an alliance with counselors who could work with at-risk youth coming to their church. Another congregation became the gathering place for all the organizations in town working with various aspects of children's health care. Another discovered restaurants willing to donate various kinds of soups for the meal served by the church. Another partnered with the marine biologists at the local aquarium who helped the church provide a series of retreats for college students called "Blue Theology." (See Appendix J for an Asset Inventory.)

THE SPIRITUAL HABIT OF GIVING THANKS

Transforming congregations let go of cynicism by cultivating the spiritual habit of gratitude. Gratitude helps them see God's provision in their midst, to focus on the good, and to give thanks for the positives that can come even out of difficult circumstances. As a result, the craving for more loosens its grip on their lives. Instead of being perpetually dissatisfied, they begin to see their resources as sufficient to the tasks that lie ahead. They begin to trust God's provision to be there, to celebrate the joys that have come to them individually during the week and to give thanks for the ways God has been working in and through the ministries of the church to change people's lives

The Gospel of John reports Jesus saying, "I came that you might have life in all its abundance." Transforming congregations discover new life in their midst when they recognize the abundance they hold in their hands. They may not have children in their church, but who *is* there? They may not have a large endowment, but how could they leverage the money they have to do some good? Those are the kinds of questions that allow transforming congregations to serve with the gifts they have and to seize opportunities as they come along.

Gratitude creates mindfulness in transforming congregations. In many congregations, mindfulness expresses itself in a very concrete activity: cleaning closets! When transforming congregations begin to trust that God's provision will continue to be there for them, they find they can let go of all those items lying around the church building that do not provide beauty or that are no longer useful. They throw out the plastic flowers that have been taking up space in the back room, give away the choir robes they no longer wear, and recycle files of old Sunday school curriculum they have not used for decades. Seeing abundance brings joy and freedom expressed by clearing out the clutter.

When transforming congregations resist the pull of the American consumer culture and chose to operate out of an economy of God's amazing and plentiful grace, they start to have more fun. They see more irony, they laugh at their mistakes and sometimes, they express humor in ways that might seem irreverent to others. Gratitude lightens the atmosphere in the church.

When transforming congregations live in gratitude, they begin to see that they do not succeed by their own striving, but by sharing in God's creative power. By regularly giving thanks they develop clarity of vision that allows them to acknowledge the reality of their situation and anticipate the ways God will work in them and through them to make a difference in the world. Giving thanks allows them to have confidence in a future they cannot see, to release their cynicism, and to become effective agents of God's transforming love in the place where they serve.

QUESTIONS FOR REFLECTION

1. When you consider your own life or the life of your congregation, would you say you live mostly in scarcity or mostly in abundance?

2. What is your perception of time? Does it drag on for you or does it go too quickly? What is something for which you would like to make more time?

3. What tangible and intangible assets are you grateful for in your life or in the life of your congregation?

4. How could you bring more gratitude into your life?

SPIRITUAL HABIT 11
COLLABORATING

The journey is too taxing to be made solo:
lacking support, the solitary traveler soon becomes weary or fear-
ful and is likely to quit the road.[125]
— Parker Palmer

During my twenties, I entered the sandcastle building contest held each year in Cannon Beach, Oregon with a team of young adults. Actually, it was more a sand sculpture contest. One year we constructed a steam locomotive; one year it was a sun with a cheery face and Mickey Mouse hands rising over some fields; another it was Cinderella's pumpkin coach pulled by six mice. On one occasion, we did make a sandcastle along with a huge dragon with his tail wrapped around it. We always decided what we would build and who would serve as our construction manager before we left for the beach; but from there on out, we improvised.

The morning began before dawn. We gathered up our buckets and shovels and trowels and found our ten foot square marked off by string and stakes in the sand. Once the signal to begin was given, we had to work quickly. Our manager stepped into our plot and drew the outline of the base in the sand while the rest of us filled buckets of water from the ocean. Then we got to work, first with shovels, then with trowels and finally with small precision knives and garden rakes.

Since we could only make use of the sand within the plot, we had to shovel out some areas in order to build up others. The pumpkin coach would need a pile of sand at least six feet high while each mouse would need only a small mound. We packed the sand down with the trowels, adding water as needed to keep the sand moist. As the sculpture took place we worked from the inside of the square to the corners so our footprints would not be visible at the end. We built the castle first and then the dragon around it.

All through the morning, our manager gave very little direction. Once the outline had been set, we simply filled it in. Each person used his or her strengths to make the creation the best it could be. The strong carried water, the artists did detail work. Those like me, with less identifiable skills, shoveled like crazy. As a team, we trusted each other. No one needed to control the process. We collaborated and cheered when an individual would come up with a creative touch to add to the sculpture. Everyone focused on the moment at hand and the pervasive sense of possibility made the work fun.

When the warning bell sounded, we finished up all the details: the doorknob on the pumpkin coach, the grill on the locomotive, the contented smile on the dragon's snout. Then the time was up and we all stepped out of the square. I do not remember if we ever won a prize, but I do remember feeling like we had done something great together. For the next two hours, tourists wandered by to admire our creation. We admired it too and congratulated ourselves for a job well done. It did not matter that by late afternoon, the tide had washed it all away.

IMPROVISING

In this age of rapid change, it is impossible for a congregation to make five-year plans like it did a few decades ago. Now, the church gives time and attention to the vision, mission, and values it will serve which set the shape for its ministry much like the outline drawn in the sand by our construction manager at the beginning of the contest. It names its purpose within God's purpose, gathers up the tools it will need, outlines the general shape the ministry will take, and then orchestrates the gifts and abilities present to accomplish the task. Along the way, the congregation improvises – making adjustments as new problems arise, as new resources appear, as new learnings emerge, and as the creative impulse inspires. The "what" stays constant while the "how" may change.

In order for each person to make a meaningful contribution to whatever ministry project is at hand, all parties must be clear about what the group is trying to accomplish; a fuzzy vision will result in a lack of participation. Likewise, it is important for everyone to commit to the same goal; if different factions work toward two different outcomes, neither will come to fruition.

Pacing also is important. Our group collaborated so well because there was a time limit that focused our energies. Transforming congregations make the most progress when they experience some urgency about what they are being called to do. When they can work hard on a ministry project for a defined amount of time and then take a rest before tackling something else, they maintain their focus. Too many projects too close together do nothing but burn people out.

When a team of people finish a ministry project, it is important to celebrate the relationships which have been forged and the good that has been done. Too many times, a congregation moves on to the next thing without taking a moment to savor what it has done. Naming even small successes can have a motivational impact on the congregation's attitude and willingness to persevere in times ahead.

THE SPIRITUAL HABIT OF COLLABORATION

When congregations are small, they may feel helpless to address the great needs of the world; but they do not need to work alone. Organizations that work in foreign countries tell us mission is always a collaborative effort. We are stronger together. Overseas mission work is often accomplished ecumenically with indigenous churches or with non-governmental organizations which have a proven history of fiscal responsibility, low administrative costs, and cultural sensitivity. In the United States, transforming congregations are learning how to work with secular partners such as social service agencies and with religious partners in order to engage in effective mission in their own communities.

One transforming congregation in a Detroit suburb joined forces with other churches and faith communities in the greater metro area to identify the three most pressing issues facing their neighborhoods. They formed interest groups around those three areas. The groups met to better understand the dimensions of the issues; over time, each group decided on an action to take. Some chose to engage in a hands-on project; some decided to lobby their elected representatives; some tried to garner support from voters for a ballot initiative. When they were finished with their work, the groups came back together to report what had been accomplished and to celebrate the transformation that was coming about because of what they had done together.

Another transforming congregation formed a coalition of downtown churches and partnered with a faith-based community organization to advocate at city council meetings for people without housing. They offered to provide space in their building to a community organization with a good track record in moving people off the street, through transitional housing, and into their own homes. In return, that organization secured grants that allowed the transforming congregation to remodel their restrooms and vacant classrooms so they could turn one wing of their building into transitional housing for nine people.

Partnership can broaden the church's effectiveness. But those who have served as missionaries in other countries will caution transforming congregations to choose their partners well. When looking for other ecumenical colleagues, faith-based organizations, or secular groups with which to work, they advise doing careful research to make sure those partners hold the same values as the church. Good partners will not only be committed to the same goals as the transforming congregation; they also will be committed to its same methods of achieving those goals. If a transforming congregation selects its partners carefully, the church will not be embarrassed by others' actions and it will maintain the integrity of its public witness.

LEADERSHIP TEAMS

In the past, congregational pastors were called to preach, to teach, to administer the sacraments, to visit the sick and the homebound, and to counsel those who needed help. It was assumed most of their week would be taken up with tasks which kept them in their study: writing a sermon, preparing for worship or advising individuals who stopped by the church office. It was assumed the members of the congregation would be the primary focus of their ministry: they were to provide services for the members of the church.

Yet in transforming congregations, pastors spend much more time giving spiritual leadership to the change process itself. They focus on equipping key lay leaders to grow in trust and hope, to help the congregation to identify a common vision, to discern the guidance of the Spirit, and to facilitate the building of relationships with neighbors. Those lay leaders and the pastor work together much like our sandcastle building construction crew. As a team, they keep the church focused on its vision, keep it true to its values, and keep it moving forward through strategic actions. They never lose sight of what they are trying to create together and they make use of the diversity of gifts among them to accomplish their mission. They work hard. They have fun. They focus on the present and are not overly obsessed with how their efforts will survive into the future.

In transforming congregations, leadership teams meet frequently to talk about what the Spirit seems to be doing in the congregation and to notice where the Spirit seems to be guiding the church to go. They keep their own sand moist by engaging daily in the spiritual habit of prayer, and practice the spiritual habit of discernment in their personal lives. They discipline themselves to open their minds to new understandings, to open their hearts to the plight of their neighbors, and to open their wills by setting aside their own agenda in order to seek God's new creation.

The leadership teams tend to their own growth and development as life-long learners. They know who they are. Instead of trying to please others (living from the outside in), they practice self-awareness (living from the inside out). They are made up of people of integrity and authenticity who seek the good of the whole community rather than pursuing their own self-gratification. Those team members have the ability to live with the ambiguity of not being able to see the whole future mapped out and planned. They are willing to trust that one step will lead to the next. They can improvise.

Leadership teams in transforming congregations do not lose their nerve when the going gets rough. They are curious and know how to ask open and honest questions for which they have no good answers. They check out their assumptions. They respond thoughtfully to challenges instead of attacking others, caving in, or getting defensive. They make choices. If they end up making a bad decision, they learn from their mistake, they choose again, and keep moving forward. (See Appendix G for guidelines for making a ministry plan.)

Members of leadership teams in transforming congregations do their part, but no one person or group of people over-functions. They understand those in the congregation will have more ownership in plans which they help to make. They share power and encourage individuals to find creative ways to participate in the congregation's shared vision. They create within the church an expectation that each person will contribute in some way, and they hold individuals and groups accountable for completing the tasks they have agreed to do.

Transformational leadership teams spend time looking at the whole picture rather than always getting caught up in the daily tasks demanding their time and attention. They have the ability to describe the current reality, to give voice to what is going on so the whole congregation can begin to see in new ways. In times of increased anxiety, transformational leaders help the congregation grow in its capacity to withstand discomfort, complexity, and ambiguity. They help the church focus on the resources they have rather than on the resources they lack. They are cheerleaders for hope.

Transformational leadership teams are open and transparent about their communication. They do not keep secrets. Members of those teams speak for themselves without assuming everyone will agree with them. They encourage individuals within the church to talk to each other rather than about each other. They do not allow misinformation to go unchecked. They try to be as clear as possible about collective decisions and move forward with those decisions even in the face of complaints, criticism, or gossip meant to derail plans which have been made by the church community.

Leadership teams in transforming congregations offer a style of governance that provides an alternative to the behaviors of control and escape which are encouraged by the American consumer culture. They are flexible, reflective, and creative about how they handle issues which arise. They celebrate the differences present in the congregation which give it vitality and spice, and discourage those behaviors which insist everyone must act and feel alike. They challenge the church to grow and change rather than trying to maintain the comfort of individuals within the church.

By the way they function with each other, members of transformational leadership teams show they can disagree and still find commonality in a shared purpose. In times of conflict, they are not afraid to take a stand. They respond graciously and truthfully when they are questioned. Through their leadership, they model the values of mutuality, collaboration, and deep listening which encourage people to collaborate as a team.

Teams of leaders in transforming congregations are good at gathering people together and helping them listen to each other. They can lead groups to create ministry plans and to name the strategic actions needed to accomplish those plans. They can shepherd those strategic actions through to their completion and they can help groups celebrate how lives have been transformed through what they have been able to accomplish together.

One team of congregational leaders held a neighborhood meeting. "We've got a vacant lot next to our building that is increasingly becoming a place of drug activity in our community. We'd like turn it into something else and we need your ideas." One man talked about an organization that created "Miracle Fields" for Special Olympics. "It's a baseball field and stadium seats all outfitted for those with special needs." The church donated the land. The Miracle Field organization built the ball park. Volunteers signed up to take tickets, to sell concessions, and to clean the stands after each game. On opening day, there was not a dry eye in the house. The church and community celebrated what they had accomplished together as one young man with no legs "ran" the bases on a four-wheeled scooter after hitting a home run.

QUESTIONS FOR REFLECTION

1. When have you been part of a team that created something together? What was it like?

2. What are the behaviors of healthy congregations? Where do you see those behaviors being lived out in your own life or in the life of the church?

3. What skills do you think will be needed for the church of the future?

4. What dangers and opportunities are created when professional clergy serve alongside lay people who have multiple levels of skill and expertise?

SPIRITUAL HABIT 12
CHOOSING

It is I who must begin.[126]

— Vaclav Havel

During the 1980s, many church leaders began adopting business practices as the means of focusing a congregation's energies, planning its work, and accomplishing its aims. They set goals, identified measurable objectives, and then created action plans to move toward anticipated outcomes. They understood the "product" of a good church was its programs, and if the church wanted to compete with other organizations vying for people's time, those programs had to be excellent. They tried to meet the needs of their customers (current members) while also striving to secure a larger market share (new members).

Alan Roxburgh notes back then the church was structured like a corporation with a headquarters (denominational office), district offices (middle judicatories) and local outlets (congregations).[127] The experts at headquarters produced training manuals that spelled out the organizational principles and standards of success. District offices trained congregational leaders in those principles so the quality of the church's worship, programs, and activities would improve. They hoped that improvement would motivate those who had never been part of the church to become members and those who had left the church to return.

During my thirties, I was one of the middle judicatory managers who trained congregations in the latest tools of the trade. I assisted leaders to craft mission statements designed to communicate their purpose and to brainstorm ideas about what their congregations might do next. We covered the walls of fellowship halls and retreat centers with newsprint displaying goals and objectives designed to make the church larger and stronger. Then

I worked with those leaders to determine specific objectives and helped them develop action plans to achieve those objectives.

But church planning has changed since then. It used to be that leaders set goals and objectives for the next five or ten years; now churches take one action, reflect on that action, learn from what they did right and what they did wrong, and decide on their next immediate step. In the past, leaders focused their goals and objectives inwardly on improving the church; now they focus them outwardly with the hope of transforming the lives of those in the neighborhood. In former times, the only people in the room during the planning process were members of the church; now partners from the neighborhood are there as well.

All of that does not mean, however, that planning cannot be strategic. Transforming churches still intentionally identify a desired outcome. They still choose to do something to achieve those goals. They still decide how they will fund their plan. The difference is, the strategies they choose are more short-term than they used to be, and after each step, the congregation takes time to reflect on what it learned and to celebrate what was accomplished before deciding on the next course of action. (See Appendix K for a process for choosing.)

Sometimes transforming congregations choose to create a mission plan that addresses the physical needs of the human body such as having enough nutritious food, clean water, shelter, and clothing. Sometimes they choose to focus on safety needs such as protection from harm and disease. Sometimes they choose to attend to care needs such as the need to love and to be loved. Sometimes they choose to concentrate on creative needs such as the need to work, to play, to make things and to make a difference. Sometimes they choose to deal with spiritual needs such as the need to connect with the sacred, to connect with the authentic Self, to connect with neighbors, and to connect with the earth. The operative concept is that transforming congregations choose and then implement their mission plan.

THE DETOUR OF DITHERING

It can be hard for congregations to decide which action they will take. They may be able to articulate their purpose, name their values, and talk about how they experience the power and the presence of the Spirit, but they dither when it comes to making a choice about how to engage in God's mission.

Some congregations avoid committing themselves to action because they have spent so much of their life and ministry funding others to do mission on their behalf. It is hard for them to muster up the courage to go outside the safety of their sanctuary, to actually meet their neighbors. They are nervous about building relationships with those who live around the church building and working with partners to carry out the mission of the church. They may feel guilty about not wanting to risk, but that guilt usually is not enough to motivate them to move outside the familiar comfort of what they know as church.

Some congregations avoid taking action because the individuals do not want to spend that much time on the practice of their faith. Caught up in the busyness of the American consumer culture's lifestyle, they want to be able to come to church for one hour on Sunday morning in order to get recharged for the week ahead. Anything beyond that minimal commitment is asking too much.

Some congregations avoid engaging in mission because they continue to harbor the belief that the church will be able to attract new people to come inside without having to do the uncomfortable work of going outside the congregation into the neighborhood. Even though there is much evidence to support the claim that the church-going era is over, they continue to wish the right new program, the right new building improvement, the right new advertising slogan will draw new people who will want to become part of the worshiping congregation.

Some congregations avoid making a decision about what they will do in mission because they do not want to cause conflict in the church. Some faction of the church may not want the church hall used by outside groups; another may not want the church's money spent on ministries that do not look like they are going to produce new church members who will tithe to the budget. Rather than stir up controversy, the congregation refuses to choose a common focus.

Some congregations dither rather than choosing because they are afraid of being wrong. They are so focused on making the perfect decision that they can make no decision at all. So they talk and talk and talk about what they might do but never really commit to a course of action.

THE SPIRITUAL HABIT OF CHOOSING

Transforming congregations learn to choose and choose again. They don't have to get it right the first time around. They can gain insight from any action they take and that insight will aid them opting to take the next step into the future. Transforming congregations acknowledge that when they act with courage, some people may decide to leave, but they would rather decide to do something than to remain lukewarm about everything. Transforming congregations do not obsess about those who complain about the strategic steps the church chooses to take; they focus on the part they can play in making God's New Creation a reality.

Transforming congregations often notice that when they do commit to a course of action, the Spirit gives them fresh insights, further opportunities, and new partners. They discover the truth of the Irish saying:

When you get to the end of all the light you know and it's time
to step into the darkness of the unknown,
faith is knowing that one of two things shall happen:
either you will be given something solid to stand on,
or you will be taught to fly.[128]

It is only after they choose to take a strategic action that they discover the resources to implement their intentions.

Some congregations make a decision by voting; but many churches learn to choose through the process of discernment. Discernment, as it is used in everyday language, has to do with sifting through the information we've been given in order to decide a course of action. In the church, discernment describes the prayerful process of making a choice in light of the inspiration, leading, and guidance of the Spirit.

Discernment can be practiced by individuals or by groups. When transforming congregations make use of discernment as a decision-making tool, they place their choices in the context of God's transforming activity, assuming that they are called to something larger than self-interest and partisanship. Through discernment, they imagine not just what they want to do, but how they might share in God's New Creation through the choices they make.

The Book of Acts tells about one of the first times the church entered into a discernment process in order to choose a course of action. It began with Paul and Barnabas framing a question that arose because of the growing number of Gentiles who were becoming Christian. They asked, "Must one be circumcised according to the custom of Moses to be saved?"[129] The Pharisees offered a conservative viewpoint based on tradition. Peter offered another opinion, calling on the gathered body to reflect on its personal experience and to recall its mission.[130] Paul and Barnabas reflected on the issue out of their own experience on the mission field, reflecting on the ways they felt God's Spirit working through them in their ministry among the Gentiles.[131] James recalled a passage from the Bible that seemed to speak to the issue at hand and then made a preliminary statement about what he believed God was calling the church to do.[132] The Elders and Apostles affirmed his insight and took action by writing a letter. At the end, their discernment was confirmed by feelings of freedom, joy, and peace.[133]

In the 16th Century, the founder of the Jesuit order, Ignatius of Loyola, developed a process of discernment modeled after the story in Acts.

1. **Clearly state the question before the congregation and name the core values** the church hopes to serve by what they choose to do.
2. **Let go** of personal preferences.

3. **Consider stories from the Bible,** from personal experience, and from others beyond the church that can inform the discernment process.
4. **Name all possible choices** that will serve the core values the church has identified.
5. **Choose** the option on which the Spirit seems to rest.

Transforming congregations often follow those five movements of discernment when they are trying to make a decision about what to do next.

One small church located in an urban neighborhood found itself in the middle of a discernment process almost by accident.[134] It all began when the city delivered a mandate: clean out the blackberry bushes on the vacant lot behind the church or face a hefty fine. The bushes had become a catch-all for neighborhood garbage and a possible breeding ground for rats. Something had to be done within the next three months. So the chair of the board called for a congregational forum to discuss the church's options.

As church participants talked together, they shaped the question before them by exploring all facets of the issue. From the old-timers in the church, they learned about the dream that vacant lot had once held for the congregation. They had hoped one day they would grow large enough to erect a large sanctuary on the property. From those in the neighborhood, they heard complaints about the cars taking up the available street parking on Sunday morning and about the unsightly mess of brambles and trash on the vacant lot. But the neighbors were also concerned a new parking lot would turn out to be a place for drug activity. From participants of the congregations who had trouble walking, they heard how hard it was to have to park so far away from the front door before worship. Finally, it became clear what question was facing the church: "What is God calling us to do with our vacant lot in light of our parking problem?"

Next, those at the congregational forum discussed the principles they believed should guide their decision:

•   We want to be a good neighbor to our community.

- We want our building to be easily accessible to all people.
- We want to be good stewards of the land entrusted to us.

Several weeks went by while members of the congregations and neighbors talked together about their concerns and dreams for the vacant lot. By the time the issue reached the agenda of the board meeting, it was clear they did not have consensus. So the board took several minutes of silence as a time of letting go. At the end, the members joined in prayer, asking to be open to God's will for the church. Then they were ready to consider all the possibilities available to them.

Together they retold the story of Jeremiah who bought a field as a way of showing he was invested in the future of Judah, even though its leaders were being marched off to exile.[135] They remembered the faith of those who had purchased the vacant lot as an inheritance for their congregation. They heard the story of the neighborhood youth who had no real place to play. They listened to the frustration of the church members who had been doing the hard work of removing the blackberry brambles each year with rented equipment.

From their sharing, they came up with two possible directions they could take and created a task group to research each one:

- Sell the property and use the money to create more parking spaces in front of the church building.
- Pave the lot so it could provide parking on Sundays and also serve as a basketball court for neighborhood youth during the week.

The task group looked at costs, zoning laws, and liability exposure. Then they reported their findings to the board: the city would not allow new parking in front of the church and the cost of paving the lot was prohibitive because of the permits needed to assure proper drainage. From their research, it was apparent new possibilities would need to be generated. So the leadership went back to the drawing board.

They read studies about how the number of parking spaces relates to church growth. They considered how many spaces could be created in a gravel lot. They learned about the environmental impact of oil seepage into ground water. They talked and struggled and prayed together. But, ultimately, it was the Bible story of Jeremiah that led them to their decision.

"You know, I was thinking about that story," one of the board members said. "It was Jeremiah's dream that one day that land could be cultivated. I know the city sponsors a Pea Patch program. They divide the land into ten by ten foot lots that people of the neighborhood who live in apartments can farm. The city gets the soil ready and provides the water. The people do the work and harvest their own crop. In the process, the garden becomes a neighborhood gathering spot where community is formed. Maybe the folks who live around here would feel like they had more of a future if they had a little bit of land they could call their own."

There was silence in the room and then a kind of gentle murmuring as those on the board considered the possibility of leasing their land to the city for a dollar so it could be turned into a Pea Patch. It was an idea that would honor their principles of neighborliness and stewardship, but what about their value of accessibility?

"Well, what if those of us who are able-bodied make it a point to park a few blocks away from the church building on Sunday morning so we don't inundate the neighborhood with cars. The walk would do us good! Then we could reserve the whole block in front for those with limited mobility." Would people in the church make the effort to park and walk? The board decided the plan was worth a try.

One year later, the vacant lot was filled with a patchwork of gardens reflecting the international diversity of the farmers. Church participants consistently parked some distance from the front door. In fact, many enjoyed parking on the street the garden faced just so they could see the changes taking place from week to week. Sometimes they struck up conversations with those who were working and sometimes they just admired the beautiful flowers and vegetables. Meanwhile, the older members of the congregation enjoyed the red-carpet treatment they were getting on Sunday morning, driving right up to the front door to park.

The practice of discernment takes time. That means it is simply impractical to utilize the process to make all the decisions that face a church in any given year. Over a twelve month period, congregations generally enter into discernment concerning only one significant issue, or at the most two, that are central to the church's life and mission. Yet discernment can be a useful tool for congregations choosing to take strategic action for the sake of the world.

QUESTIONS FOR REFLECTION

1. How has your congregation changed the way it plans together?

2. When have you or your congregation avoided making a decision? What kept you from choosing?

3. Has your congregation ever engaged in the movements of discernment? What happened?

4. What decision is facing your congregation right now? How will you choose what do next?

FRESH EXPRESSIONS

*It may be that when we no longer know
what to do that we come to our real work,
and that when we no longer know
which way to go, we have begun our real journey.*[136]
— Wendell Berry

"Let's hike up Mount Baldy," my husband suggested. We can see the mountain from our dining room window but we had never gone to the top. So we packed a lunch and our ten hiking essentials and set out. We drove to the trailhead, parked, and started walking along the easy trail that followed the stream. The path was forested and the way was clear. But after a couple of miles, the trail entered a meadow. Where did the trail go from there? We couldn't see. The only thing we knew was that our destination was in the upward direction so we kept climbing. My dad used to call it "gullywumping" – finding the way where there is no way. For the next several hours we made our own paths up the slope, keeping our goal in sight. Eventually we arrived at a place where we could see the whole valley laid out below our feet. We sat down to rest and enjoyed the view.

Many congregations that decide to embark on the transforming journey find themselves on a path blazed by others that have gone before them. But there comes a time when transforming congregations discover they cannot see the way forward and they simply must gullywump. Those congregations are trying out new ways of being church for a time such as this. Some are starting new communities of faith and some are transforming themselves into fresh expressions that can tell the old story in new ways. Those fresh expressions likely only hint at what the church in a hundred years will look like; but as congregations continue to learn, to grow, and to evolve over time, they will find the forms needed to speak to new generations not yet born.

THE WORSHIPING CONGREGATION

It is quite possible corporate worship as we know it today may diminish in importance later in this century. However, over the next few decades the primary form of the church likely will continue to be weekly gatherings of the congregation for the purpose of singing, praying, listening to the reading of scripture, giving testimony and sharing in the sacrament of communion. The seating may be set up like an auditorium or in the round with most of the leadership coming from a podium up front or in the center of the community. Yet there will be no one style which will characterize worship. Some services will follow a very traditional liturgy; others will be more freeform. Some services will include guitars, drums and a projection screen; others will involve brass and organ. Some will be wildly joyful; others will be quiet and reflective.

Musical selections will not be limited to "contemporary" or "traditional." They will reflect a wide range of styles from many cultures. The strength of worship will not lie in the entertainment value of what happens up front; rather it will come from the large number of participants who contribute to the service over time. Its dynamism will not depend on the professional excellence of the various worship elements; rather, it will emerge from the feeling of celebration and joy that permeates the service.

Because individuals who participate in the worship life of transforming congregations will have an active daily prayer life, images and words they encounter in the corporate worship will connect them with experiences of the Spirit they have had during the week. A phrase in a song, in a reading, or in the proclamation may well remind them of a time in which they experienced a call upon their lives, a clarity of purpose, or an impetus to take compassionate action on behalf of someone else. Those moments of resonance will be what infuse the worship service with a sense of integrity and power.

Worship in transforming congregations will offer reminders of what the congregation is trying to become. Together, worshipers may recite the church's vision statement as part of the service. The readings or the proclamation may call to mind the global context in which the church ministers, making use of songs from other cultures, other languages and utilizing images from nature that evoke wonder, awe, and gratitude. A time of extended silence during the service may offer Sabbath for individual reflection, meditation or contemplative prayer, countering the noise and busyness of daily life. The service likely will include testimonies of "God moments" worshipers experienced during the week.

Transforming congregations will make wide use of symbols and metaphors during worship. Visual media including film and video clips may be shown as part of the church's proclamation. Story will also play a key role in the service. The meta-narrative of God's New Creation often will be given prominence; but that larger story will take its place alongside more contemporary stories of how people both inside and outside the congregation live out that vision.

Although there may be a "children's sermon" during worship in transforming congregations, school-age children and youth will be integrally incorporated into the whole of the service and not only in that set-aside time. They will be invited to contribute prayers, to serve as readers and to share testimony alongside the adults. They will be asked to contribute artwork, photographs, original musical compositions, and poetry. They will be encouraged to share their musical talents, not as entertainment for the church but as an offering of who they are before God.

Creative, expectant participation will permeate the worship service, no matter the style. Often there will be several lay leaders, trained in the art of drama or interpretive reading, who will present scripture and/or poetry as part of the liturgy. The screen at the front of the sanctuary may showcase original art pieces or photography by congregational participants. Musicians will share original songs.

THE SMALL GROUP CONGREGATION

Some congregations in the 21st Century will consist of a collection of small groups meeting around dining room tables, in the back rooms of coffee houses, in pubs, in schools, in libraries, and in wineries. Some congregations will be one small group; others will be networks of small groups meeting periodically to worship together. Those small groups will focus on the personal growth and development of their members. They will hold to the practices of hospitality which make for trustworthy community. They will covenant to walk with each other through the journey of transformation.

Most small group gatherings will begin with sharing food. A simple meal or some snacks create a relaxed atmosphere where people more naturally form relationships with each other. Next may come a brief time of checking in with each other. In the style of the United Methodist tradition, participants may be asked to answer the question, "How is it with your soul?" After that, the group may take a time for centering, for contemplative prayer or for gathering themselves into the space.

Imagine such a group. A story, a poem, a passage of scripture, a video clip, a piece of art introduces the theme of the gathering. Through a time of journaling, solitude, silence, or artwork that theme develops more fully. Pairs or triads gather for sharing and deep listening. The whole group joins back together so individuals may comment on any insights gained through the process. The small group concludes with a time of singing, prayer, worship, or communion around the circle.

In Montana where there are small population centers spread out across a vast landscape, the Christian Church (Disciples of Christ) is forming small groups called Open Circles. An Open Circle is a spiritual community of seven to thirty people in which individuals can explore the deep questions of life. Steeped in the forms of community developed by Parker Palmer, Open Circles are places of deep listening. In an Open Circle, people of varied opinions and backgrounds come together to eat, reflect and pray, gaining courage from each other and learning to discern and trust the voice of God's Spirit.

Open Circles meet regularly in a home or in a quiet room of a rent-free public space such as a coffee shop, restaurant, or bookstore—any place where people can sit in a circle, speak confidentially, and hear easily what is being shared. Two lay volunteers who live in the community where the Open Circle meets lead the gatherings. Once each quarter, Open Circles within a larger geographical area participate together in a thematic retreat to build relationships with a wider community, to worship together, to study scripture, to engage in theological dialogue, to create, to connect with nature, to rest and to play.

Open Circles composed of church participants and non-participants may form as part of the ministry of a larger congregation. An Open Circle also may take shape as a satellite of an established congregation. An Open Circle may relate to other Open Circles within a particular geographic area.

Most Open Circle participants are those who would call themselves "spiritual but not religious." Some have been deeply wounded by the church and some have never been part of the church at all. In an Open Circle, each person is given the opportunity to connect to an inner source of wisdom we call Spirit who can teach, guide, comfort, and challenge. An Open Circle helps its participants to make that connection, to trust that connection and to ground their lives in its power and presence.

Open Circle participants are encouraged to cultivate a habit that will help them grow spiritually. They also are encouraged to participate in mission in their own communities. Often, Open Circle participants partner with individuals from established congregations and people from the community who are interested in making a difference in the world.

MISSIONAL COMMUNITIES

A Missional Community is a group of 30-50 people committed to accomplishing one mission. Individuals in a Missional Community may all be part of one congregation or they may be part of many congregations or no congregation at all. What binds them together is their commitment to building relationships with their neighbors and identifying a specific action which will cause their neighborhood to more clearly resemble God's New Creation.

Whether residential or community-based, a Missional Community will work with partners in order to accomplish their goals. They may partner with other groups, organizations or congregations that can offer funding, staffing, space or expertise. Those partner groups will always be in on the mission planning from the beginning and will always be treated with mutuality as the plan is carried out.

Sometimes a Missional Community will work with a particular population such as children or youth, people without a home, or people with addictions. In some of those situations, the missional group may actually sponsor the formation of another group as a means for accomplishing their mission. They may call leaders to create a worship service designed for another ethnic population. They may call leaders to create a recovery group. They may call leaders to create a support group for at-risk teens. In each case, those leaders may need to have specialized training in order to be effective in the ministry.

One missional group in a rural community decided to make food sustainability the focus of their mission. Together, they formed a food-cooperative so they could buy in bulk from local farmers and save on the fuel it would take to truck their food from far away. "We gave up some variety," one participant said, "in order to buy closer to home." Over time, that group began to get active in other issues such as saving small farms from corporate take-over and raising concerns about genetically altered grain. They even began looking at communities in other countries who were way ahead of them when it came to sustainable agriculture.

OFF-SITE CONGREGATIONS

One big challenge facing historic Protestant congregations is the large portion of the budget which is being consumed by heating and repairing aging buildings instead of being used for mission and ministry. Congregations in the future may solve that problem by turning their building from a liability into an asset. Some may rent their building space to other organizations or other churches to offset their upkeep costs. Some may sell their building and rent back just the space they need for their congregation. Some may spend their endowment earnings to fix up the facility so their building actually can serve as the kind of space they need to carry out their ministry to the neighborhood. Some may leave their building behind and meet in homes or public space.

Those off-site congregations may gather in grange halls, schools, museums, wineries, libraries, or movie theaters. They may make use of retreat centers and yoga studios. Sometimes they will gather at the worksite of a Habitat Home or other neighborhood project. Making use of public space may allow them to connect with those who are skittish about entering a church building, either because they have had bad experiences with church or because they are leery of church as an institution.

Other off-site congregations will build or re-purpose a building to make room for multiple ministries to be housed. Those multi-purpose church buildings may contain low income housing, office space for non-profit groups, worship space, and places for small groups to meet. Others may run coffee shops or bookstores where they can build community or host theological conversation. Still others may create venues where artists can showcase their work or musicians can share their compositions. Such forms of church will have little expectation people will come join the church; rather, as servants of Christ, they will join the world.

One congregation in Washington was down to just a few older people in worship when they decided to let go of everything for the sake of reaching out in mission to the next generation. They could see that they were living in a time when many younger people were skeptical about walking into a church building so the congregation decided to sell their building and to use their resources to build a new facility to house a non-profit café, pub, community spot, and music venue where younger people would feel at home. They also were concerned about soldiers returning from combat who were having trouble finding jobs and housing, so they made sure the new building would have office space for the Veteran's Affairs Administration and apartments for veterans.

Now the old pews serve as booth seating and a wall hanging made up of the old seasonal pulpit and lectern cloths graces one wall of the cafe. Volunteers staff the cash register, cook, and wait tables. Veterans and others from the community gather for music, food, and drink. Young and old alike showcase original musical compositions. Thirty percent of all proceeds go to outreach ministries. A small new church start holds a service in the café on Sunday evening. Worship, fellowship, and mission are all taking place in the new building, but they look different than they did before.

CYBER-CHURCHES

It is hard to know how technology will change the church of the future; yet it is safe to say it will play a role in shaping how future generations will engage in being church together. Already on-line chat rooms and threaded conversations are places where people discuss theology and planning takes place via video-conferencing. Many congregations already find resources on line. Some rural churches tap into the worship services of larger congregations. Youth scattered in isolated communities meet together with their adult sponsor in a video chat room for youth group. Individuals in churches keep up-to-date with prayer requests and pastoral care needs through social media sites. Congregations connect with mission partners across the globe through interactive internet programs. Children learn Bible stories from DVDs. Adult classes make use of on-line clips which allow them to listen to trusted scholars. Churches attend continuing education events and denominational meetings through streaming video.

Generations who have had to learn technology may be quick to say that virtual interactions do not replace face-to-face relationships; but for younger people who have grown up with technology as a native language, that may not be the case. Younger generations may find new uses for the technological tools they have now and they may develop new tools in the future that will allow them to grow spiritually, to connect as community, and to make the world different.

New Models of Pastoral Leadership

Over the last few decades, the historic Protestant church has gotten used to paying one full-time seminary-trained ordained minister to serve the needs of one congregation. That will no longer be the norm in the 21st Century. Most congregations will be smaller so they will not be able to afford a full-time pastor; responsibilities will be carried out by teams. New models already are emerging that make use of ordained ministers in a variety of ways:

- One pastor giving oversight to several lay-led congregations
- One bi-vocational pastor serving one congregation
- One pastor preaching for multiple congregations via video or internet streaming
- One pastor preaching and leading worship for several yoked congregations at various times during the week
- One pastor serving as a missionary to a certain population or neighborhood
- A team of pastors giving oversight to several churches operating as one parish

As the church finds its way into the future, the role of clergy will shift even more than it already has. Although some ministers will preach and lead worship, many will give their time to training lay people as worship leaders and small group facilitators. Although some will offer pastoral care, that care will extend beyond the members of the church into the neighborhood. Although some will teach, that teaching will focus on equipping individuals to serve in various roles both inside and outside the church. The sacramental tasks of baptizing, leading in communion, presiding at weddings and funerals increasingly will be shared with people beyond those who are ordained.

In the future, ministers will receive varying amounts of education and training through an assortment of methods. Some will continue to graduate from seminary with a Master of Divinity degree, but more of their coursework likely will be completed online. Some will be apprenticed and mentored by a large teaching

church. Some will receive training in the practical aspects of ministry much like EMTs receive in the medical field. Some will engage
in specialized education in areas such as community organizing,
social justice ministries, spiritual direction, small group leadership,
adult education, or strategic missional planning.

OVERSIGHT MINISTRY

In the future, there may be more call for the oversight ministry
of judicatories, not less. As the number of lay leaders increases so
will the need to protect the church through criminal background
checks and boundary training in sexual ethics. As the amount and
style of education for ministry becomes more varied, it will be even
more important to make sure the church is being led by spiritually
mature people who can read and interpret the Bible, think theologically, provide excellence in transformational leadership, and who
know how to create trustworthy community.

Judicatories in the future may take on a larger financial management role making grants to groups who want to start new
ministries or expand successful endeavors. Since worship in the
future may take place more in clusters of churches rather in one
lone congregation, there will be a need for oversight ministers to
plan, orchestrate, and coordinate services for a geographic area.
Judicatory leaders may find themselves working with educational
institutions and large congregations to provide ongoing specialized
training for a variety of ministries such as spiritual formation, small
group dynamics, congregational systems, deep listening, and community development. Judicatories may also become the place where
pastors and lay leaders find peer support in groups designed to help
them keep their feet on the path of transformational leadership.

Judicatories likely will discover themselves also helping congregations create a basic philanthropy tool kit. Part of their role may
be aiding a congregation in analyzing a social problem, doing due
diligence on organizations or agencies that may serve as potential
partners to congregations engaging in mission, evaluating the success or failure of those potential partners, and investigating how
much overhead is paid for with donor dollars.

All this is to say, the leadership for the 21ˢᵗ Century church will look a lot like the image of the body with many parts put forth by the Apostle Paul in a letter to the church at Corinth.

> *Now there are varieties of gifts, but the same Spirit; and there are varieties of services, but the same Lord; and there are varieties of activities, but it is the same God who activates all of them in everyone.*
>
> *To each is given the manifestation of the Spirit for the common good.* (1 Corinthians 12:4-5)

There will be many ways to serve, yet there will be a role for each part of the body. Some will teach the practices of prayer, some will encourage gratitude, some will help the church learn how to be hospitable to a variety of people; some will lead congregations to discern their vocation, values, and mission. There likely will be fewer "general practitioners" and more people living out their own gifts for ministry in particular ways. There will be fewer individuals serving as solo pastors and more lay people and clergy working as teams. There will be fewer professionals paid to do the work of the church and more lay people engaged in mission with their neighbors as a part of their way of life.

Because the context of the 21ˢᵗ Century will continue to evolve, it is not possible to see all the expressions the church will take in the coming years. Yet already new forms of church are taking shape. Some look like new versions of familiar structures. Others are forms from the past that are taking on new life. Still others are models of new church that have not existed before. As these new forms continue to emerge, they will require different kinds of leaders and support. But with creativity, courage, and compassion, the church can rise to the occasion, taking whatever shape is needed to continue to bring a relevant word to new generations.

QUESTIONS FOR REFLECTION

1. What new forms of church do you see emerging?

2. Why might those fresh expressions carry potential for touching the lives of those not currently affiliated with the church?

3. What are the dangers and opportunities that might come with a congregation not being housed in a building?

4. If your congregation were to start a new church, what form would it take?

A CHURCH THAT MATTERS

Each individual Christian in each new age of the church has to make a return to the source of the Christian life. [137]
— Thomas Merton

Sowing seed is risky business. The Montana sodbusters found that out during the Dustbowl. They could do their very best, work hard, put in long hours, use the latest farming techniques the Almanac had to offer, and still everything could go wrong. Drought dried up the land. Wind blew the topsoil away. Hope wilted along with the crops, but what could they do? They quit, packed up, moved out, and moved on. As I travel across the Montana landscape, I see their deserted houses, their useless windmills, their broken-down wagons, and the ghost towns they left behind.

And yet when Jesus wanted to show what God's New Creation was like, he told a story about a resolute little farmer who went about doing what farmers do. Surely that farmer knew all the dangers out there: the bugs, the birds, the rocky soil. Surely he knew his work could end up being pointless. But he didn't stay in bed. He didn't stay at home. He went out. He strapped on his sack and went out to sow seed. [138]

Transforming congregations take risks. They fling seed all over the place, trying this and trying that, waiting to see what will grow in the new landscape of the 21st Century. Some of those risks produce fruit and some do not. But transforming congregations who find their way into the future do not give up; they keep experimenting, keep trying, and keep learning. "It may be that the most important quality a transforming congregation can have is stubbornness," one pastor said. "We were fortunate to have several younger couples who were willing to put up with the church as it was because they knew eventually it would change."

It takes a lot of perseverance over a number of years for the church to experience true transformation. There is a lot to overcome. First, a congregation must contend with the natural resistance to change that can come from within the church. Secondly, it must take seriously the public relations problem that originates outside the church. Yet, even in the face of such enormous challenges, transforming congregations persist.

The way transforming congregations participate in God's New Creation sets them apart from churches that continue to ascribe to the conventional piety of Golden Rule Christianity. Their approach to scripture and their willingness to think theologically separates them from both Fundamentalists and those Christians who seek personal wealth and prosperity. Their efforts to create safe place where individuals can explore the large questions of life contrast them with those churches characterized by judgemental-ism. Their desire to understand the voice of the Spirit and to see with the eyes of the heart distinguishes them from those who stopped learning right after graduating from Sunday school.

Those differences speak to those who have left the church, those who have been wounded by the church, and those who have never been part of the church. When that happens, there is joy! "If I had known there was a congregation like this around, I would have been here sooner," one woman exclaimed. "This is a church that matters."

THE QUALITATIVE DIFFERENCE

Those who enter into a transforming congregation may not know the history of the church's transforming journey. They may not know the church's denominational affiliation. They may not know which spiritual habits the church practices. But they do know that a transforming congregation feels different than other church-es. Here are some of the qualities that set it apart:

There is joy. Faces are open and expectant. The church cele-brates people, has fun, and laughs. It treats unexpected events as new opportunities; it greets surprise with delight.

There is affirmation. People are present to one another. Encouragement fills the air. People speak positively to and about the clergy. Leadership receives appreciation.

There is ownership. Ministry is not left to the professionals; everybody participates in some aspect of the church's mission. The budget is not underwritten by a few wealthy individuals; the financial load is shared by each person.

There is variety. Throughout the week, the congregation gathers in various configurations with others from the neighborhood for learning, sharing, praying, planning and service. Music is a mix of various styles. Prayer blends many traditions.

There is flexibility. Leadership teams are given the permission they need to be nimble in responding to changing situations. The church encourages innovation, creativity, and experimentation.

There is openness. The space is bounded enough that people feel free to be themselves. They dialogue about the Bible, theological issues and ethical dilemmas. They learn and grow and embrace new ways of doing things.

These qualities which make up the atmosphere in transforming congregations are the fruits produced by what they are becoming and what they do in response to God's claim upon their life and ministry:

1. **Transforming congregations let go of anxiety and connect with the Spirit within.** They root themselves in the power and presence of God through prayer. They discern the voice of the Spirit that speaks through symbol and metaphor. They commit themselves to grow spiritually all the days of their lives.

2. **Transforming congregations let go of personal preference and connect with a purpose larger than self-interest.** They align their mission with God's mission of peace, security, and justice for all. They engage in ministry wherever there is suffering. They frequently testify to the activity of the Spirit that works in and through their vision, mission, and core values.

3. **Transforming congregations let go of criticism and connect as authentic community.** They create safe places that welcome

the soul and allow for adult development. They integrate the stranger by forming mutual relationships. They think theologically, build capacity, and expect accountability.

4.   **Transforming congregations let go of cynicism and connect with the world in all its complexity.** They cultivate gratitude which, in turn, cultivates a sense of plenty. They open their collective heart to the wide variety of individuals who make up the human race. They choose to engage the world through strategic actions and they collaborate with each other and with partners to get the work done.

The spiritual habits cultivated by a transforming congregation are the glue that holds it together. They give the church its character and its courage and allow it to function less like an organization and more like an organism. They make it possible for the church to adapt to change. They invite the church to say yes to a whole set of behaviors and attitudes and no to another set.

It takes a great deal of vigilance for a congregation to stay on course. It must not only choose those behaviors which lead to vitality and growth but it must also leave behind those behaviors which do not serve God's purposes. It is not easy for the church to continually hold itself accountable to the task. When anxiety or fatigue strikes, there always is the temptation to slip back into familiar patterns. Diligence in the twelve spiritual habits allows transforming congregations to recognize the choices of life and death that have been set before them and to choose life so that they and their descendants may live.[139]

LEADING CHANGE

A core team of committed lay leaders and clergy within a congregation can do a lot toward helping that church transform itself so it can be an agent of transformation in the world. When individuals on the team seek solitude each day for listening prayer, their practice creates the expectation that congregational participants will also take time to connect with God's Spirit. When they engage in opportunities for personal growth, they help establish a congregational climate where life-long learning becomes the norm and participants develop the capacity to live from the inside out. When that team involves itself in gatherings where time is slowed by silence and contemplative listening and when it consistently maintains boundaries established by the congregation's behavioral covenant, congregational participants begin to trust that church can be a safe space.

During its first gatherings, the core team describes the current reality of the congregation's life and ministry from the perspective of a hypothetical guest who comes to visit. It takes courage to tell the truth about that person's experience without resorting to wishful thinking about what the team would like that person to see and feel. However, facing the reality of what is can open the door to something new.

Next, the leaders on the core team consider how they create the reality that the visitor experiences. They do not try to manipulate or escape that reality. They avoid placing blame on something or someone else for that reality. They take responsibility for their own unspoken commitments, habits, and assumptions that make the church what it is. When they are willing to really see how what they are doing contributes to the way the congregation functions, they begin to understand that they are not powerless victims; they have the ability to change the dynamics of the congregational system.[140]

Those on the core team set aside their own egos in order to open their will to the will of God. They commit themselves to God's purposes. They let go of the past in order to move into the future. Then they begin to explore what the Spirit might be calling the church to do next. What are the key questions or themes that begin to emerge? What images come to mind when they consider the future that they believe God is calling the church to create? What must they relinquish in order to bring God's vision into reality?[141]

As the core team discerns the leading of the Spirit and begins to get a hunch about the future direction of the congregation, it reflects on what it needs to learn next. The quest for new knowledge might take the team on a field trip into a new situation where it can see the seeds of the future being planted in the present. It might propel the team out into the community to interview neighbors or potential partners. It might steer the team to a piece of writing to fuel the imagination.

Then the core team prototypes a small version of the future it wants to create. That prototype is not a pilot project; rather it is a sketchy experiment that can take place within a three to four month period. Its purpose is to provide yet more learning for the core team as they continue to explore what action it will take next.

Throughout the process, the core team moves like a dancer from an inward focus on its own reflection to an outward dialogue with the other leadership structures in the church and back again. It keeps the board or the council informed about what it is doing, what it is seeing, and what it is learning. At certain points, the core team might hold a congregational forum to receive input from the larger body. At other junctures, it might ask for an official vote to move the church forward.

CHALLENGE TO THE CHURCH

This book has depicted a collage of many kinds of transforming congregations that share twelve spiritual habits. They minister in cities, in suburbs, in farmland. They come in various sizes and shapes. Your church's story may or may not actually have been told in these pages; but it is likely that you recognized your congregation. Each unique journey contains elements common to the road all transforming congregations travel. We cannot help but see in the experience of others something of our own.

That means that whether your congregation is just waking up to landscape of the 21st Century or you have been struggling with change for a long time, there are other churches who share your story. Perhaps you have made false starts, failed at what you have tried, and now you are getting tired. Perhaps something new is beginning to grow in and among you. Wherever you are on the journey, know that you are not alone, that others are traveling with you, beside you. Also know that, for all the chaos and confusion around you, you are not wandering aimlessly; you are on the path to God's New Creation which is emerging in you and before you.

Look around the area where you serve. Are there transforming congregations in your own state, county, or section of the city? What can you learn from them? What can they learn from you? Of course, it is not possible to duplicate what others have done; each congregation is unique in regard to its gifts, its context, and its call. What worked in one place cannot be lifted up and transported to another place without losing a lot in translation. But if you focus on the spiritual habits themselves, they can light your way into the future.

As you cultivate those habits within your own life and ministry, see where they will take you in your own unique location, with your own neighbors, using your own abilities. Are there some habits you already practice? How have they changed you? Are there habits which need more attention? How could you incorporate them into what you already do? As you allow the Spirit to transform your church, you may find your congregation becoming an agent of transformation in the world. As you allow the spiritual habits to light your way, you may find your congregation becoming a church that matters.

QUESTIONS FOR REFLECTION

1. Use the worksheet in Appendix L to assess how your congregation says yes and how it says no. How do you want to alter the choices you make?

2. Which congregations in your geographic area are on the transforming journey? How could you encourage each other along the road?

3. Which spiritual habits does your congregation practice? How have those habits helped you stay the course?

4. Which spiritual habits would you like to cultivate? How will you begin?

Appendix A

Which of the following spiritual habits describes your congregation?

_____Transforming congregations root themselves in the power and presence of God through prayer.

_____Transforming congregations listen to the voice of the Spirit which speaks through sign, symbol, and metaphor.

_____Transforming congregations continue to grow spiritually.

_____Transforming congregations align their purpose with God's purpose of peace, security and justice for all.

_____Transforming congregations engage in ministry where there is suffering.

_____Transforming congregations frequently testify to the activity of the Spirit that works in and through their vision, mission, and core values.

_____Transforming congregations become inclusive communities by welcoming the stranger and forming mutual relationships.

_____Transforming congregations question religious perspectives that have lost credibility and engage in robust theological dialogue about issues posed by change.

_____Transforming congregations build capacity and expect accountability.

_____Transforming congregations cultivate gratitude which helps them see God's provision of plenty in their midst.

_____Transforming congregations collaborate with other partners in order to serve God's intentions in the place where they live.

_____Transforming congregations choose to take strategic actions that heal personal, social, and environmental injuries.

Are there other spiritual habits you would add to the list?

Appendix B
Forms of Listening Prayer

Based on *Prayer and Temperament: Different Prayer Forms for Different Personality Types* by Chester P. Michael and Marie C. Norrisey

1. PRAYING WITH THE IMAGINATION: Ignatius of Loyola encouraged Christians to put themselves into a Biblical passage and to use their senses to explore the scene. What does it look like? What sounds can you hear? What can you smell? What conversations do you overhear? What happens next? What do you do? What does the Spirit say to you as a result of your immersion in that place?

2. TRANSPOSING PRAYER: Augustine of Hippo taught Christians to transpose the words of a Biblical passage to their lives. They put themselves in the place of the Biblical character and listen to the words spoken as if they are addressing their personal situation.

3. *LECTIO DIVINA* (DIVINE READING): The Benedictine tradition taught others how to read through a Biblical passage slowly, listening to the whole passage, to read through it again, listening to the word of phrase that seems to speak directly to their own lives, and then to read it again, considering what action that phrase might be guiding them to take.

4. CENTERING PRAYER: A book by a 14th Century anonymous author entitled The Cloud of Unknowing taught a form of prayer in which a person sits in silence with eyes closed and focuses on one word or phrase of their choosing that invites the presence of the sacred Spirit.

5.   CONTEMPLATIVE PRAYER: Hildegard of Bingen and others taught Christians to focus on a scene or an object from nature, allowing it to reveal to them some aspect of God's nature and purpose.

APPENDIX C
THE PRAYER OF EXAMEN

Adapted from *Ignatius of Loyola's Spiritual Exercises* by Ronald C. Greene

Where have you noticed the presence of the Spirit:

In your inner thoughts and experiences?

In your relationships and encounters with other people?

In the systems and structures of the world?

In the environment of God's creation?

APPENDIX D
A LIFE MAP

In the space below, make a spiritual map of your life, paying particular attention to the turns your journey has taken. Use color to show how you felt about each phase of your life.

Sunday School
Confirmation
    Communion

College – church   ✳

  Marriage

Children – start
   cycle again

Teaching SS – directing
   church choir

Teaching pub. sch.

Teaching Bible studies
Council – 3 churches
   Old age

Appendix E
The Already and The Not-Yet

On the left side of the table, list the characteristics of God's New Creation. On the right side of the table, list the ways you see those characteristics being lived out in your neighborhood. In the middle column list the actions that would be needed to fill the gaps.

Characteristics of God's New Creation	Actions Needed to Fill the Gap between the Vision and the Reality	How God's New Creation is Being Lived Out in Our Neighborhood

Appendix F
Formulating our Congregation's Vision, Mission, and Values

What has characterized our congregation's life and ministry through the years?

Where do we still see those characteristics in the current life and ministry of the congregation?

What is the Spirit calling to us to be?

In which part of God's New Creation is the Spirit calling us to participate?

Which of Jesus' values do we want to serve through the life and ministry of our church?

How can we communicate our congregation's vision, mission, and values to others?

Is there an image that captures our vision, mission and values?

How can we make our congregation's vision, mission, and values live?

APPENDIX G
CREATING A MINISTRY PLAN

Seeing: When we talk with neighbors, what changes do they tell us most need to take place in our neighborhood for it to more closely resemble God's New Creation?

Reflecting: What have we learned about root causes behind those needs?

Connecting: Who are the individuals and organizations that already are working to make the needed changes? What do they have to teach us?

Choosing: What action will we choose that uses our gifts to further God's work in the world?

Implementing: How will we fund and carry out that action?

Evaluating: When will we evaluate that action in order to learn from it and decide what to do next?

Celebrating: How will we celebrate what was accomplished through the action?

Appendix H
Asking Open and Honest Questions

Based on *Guidelines for Asking Open and Honest Questions* from the Center for Courage and Renewal

Ask open and honest questions. An open and honest question is one to which you cannot possibly know the answer. It has no agenda behind it.

Avoid questions with yes-no, right-wrong answers. At the same time, remember that the best questions often are simple and straight-forward.

Try not to get ahead of the speaker's language with your questions. Don't read more into what is said than what is actually said.

Ask questions that are brief and to the point rather than building a runway with rationales and background materials.

Ask questions aimed at helping the speaker explore his or her concern rather than satisfying your own curiosity.

If you aren't sure about how appropriate it is to ask a particular question, sit with it for a while and wait for clarity.

Watch the pacing of the questions, allowing some silence between the last answer and the next question. Questions that come too fast may feel aggressive.

APPENDIX I
WRITING A BEHAVIORAL COVENANT

What safe church practices do we want to put in place? (Your insurance company can provide you with suggestions.)

What boundaries will help us create emotional and spiritual safety in the congregation?

What healthy styles of communication do we expect from congregational participants?

Who is responsible for maintaining appropriate boundaries in our congregation?

What will we do if someone violates a boundary?

Appendix J
Asset Inventory

What physical resources do we have that could be used for mission?

What monetary resources to we have that could be used for mission?

What gifts of skills, talents, and gifts are present among our congregation's participants?

Who among us can offer leadership?

What good news do we have to share?

What qualities in our life and ministry have given us energy and joy?

Who are our friends and partners in the neighborhood?

Who else could help us with our mission?

APPENDIX K
A PROCESS FOR CHOOSING

Based on the *Movements of Discernment in Discerning God's Will Together: A Spiritual Practice for the Church* by Danny E. Morris and Charles M. Olsen (Herndon, VA: Alban Institute, 2012)

What is the question before us?

What are the vision and values that can guide our decision?

What is the wisdom from the Bible that can guide our decision?

What do people inside our congregation have to say about the issue before us?

What do our neighbors have to say about the issue before us?

What other voices do we need to hear?

What seem to be the best 2-3 actions we could take?

For each possible action:

- What are the advantages and disadvantages of choosing that path?

- What are the advantages and disadvantages of not choosing that path?

After praying about which action to take, is there one which seems to present itself as the right path to take?

APPENDIX L
SAYING YES AND SAYING NO

Circle the behaviors in each column that best describe the choices your congregation usually makes.

Saying No To	Saying Yes To
Clinging to what has lost its efficacy	Relinquishing what has lost its efficacy
Denying changes in the context of ministry	Adapting to changes in the context of ministry
Fearing the unknown	Trusting that God is in the unknown
Practicing religion accessed through rational thought	Practicing spirituality accessed through the marriage of reason and intuition
Arrested development	Life-long growth
Personal preference guiding vision	God's purposes guiding vision
Escaping complexities of the world	Engaging the world in all its complexities
Setting direction by listening to the most anxious voice	Setting direction by developing common vision, values, and mission
Judging others	Extending welcome
Doing for	Doing with
Creating dependence	Building capacity
Becoming cynical	Becoming grateful
Going it alone	Collaborating partners
Dithering	Risking

How would you like to make different choices as a congregation?

NOTES

PREFACE

1   Patricia O'Connell Killen and Mark Silk, *Religion and Public Life in the Pacific Northwest: The None Zone* (Walnut Creek, CA: AltaMira Press, 2004).

INTRODUCTION

2   Charles DuBos, *Approximations* (Paris; Librarre Plon, 1922).

3   Howard Gardner names verbal intelligence, logical intelligence, spatial intelligence, kinesthetic intelligence, musical intelligence, interpersonal intelligence, intrapersonal intelligence, intuitive intelligence, and naturalist intelligence in his book now in its third edition: *Frames of Mind: the Theory of Multiple Intelligences* (New York: Basic Books, 2011).

4   Joseph Stiglitz, *The Price of Inequality: How Today's Divided Society Endangers Our Future* (New York: W. W. Norton and Company, 2012).

5   "The State of Consumption Today" by Worldwatch Institute, Washington DC: worldwatch@worldwatch.org, 2013.

6   Nancy T. Ammerman, "Spiritual Journeys in the American Mainstream," *Faith Communities* 22 no. 1, January-February, 1997, 11-15.

7   5 million copies of Norman Vincent Peale's book, *Power of Positive Thinking* have sold in America. (Wikipedia.org, 2008).

8   Roger Fink and Rodney Stark, *The Churching of America* (Rutgers University Press, 1994).

9   Thomas Byrne Edsall, "The Morality Gap in American Politics", *The Atlantic Monthly*, January, 2003.

10   Barry A. Kosmin and Ariela Keysar, "American Religious Identification Survey" (ARIS), Hartford CT: Program on Public Values, 2009. The irrelevancy of the church is also discussed in David Kinnaman and Gabe Lyons, *UnChristian* (Grand Rapids, MI: Baker Books, 2007), 121-126.

SPIRITUAL HABIT 1

11   Mark Nepo, *The Exquisite Risk: Daring to Live an Authentic Life* (New York: Harmony Books, 2005), 14.

12   Michael E. Derr and Murry Bowen, *Family Evaluation: An Approach Based on Bowen Theory* (New York: W.W. Norton, 1988), 112.

13 A more complete analysis of human reactivity to anxiety can be found in Peter L. Steinke, *Congregational Leadership in Anxious Times* (Herndon, VA: Alban Institute, 2006), 5-13.

14 This classic theory of why people cut themselves off from new learning was first described in Milton Rokeach et al, *The Open and Closed Mind* (New York: Basic Books, 1960), 284.

15 One example is found in Luke 3:22 when the Spirit descends on Jesus at his baptism like a dove.

16 Numbers 11:2-5; Acts 2:3.

17 Luke 4:14 is one example.

18 Isaiah 44:3.

19 1 Samuel 10:6 is one example.

20 Ephesians 2:22; I Peter 2:5.

21 1 Kings 18:12; Ezekiel 3:12-14; Revelation 17:3, 21:10.

22 Paul uses the phrase "in Christ" no less than 15 times in his letters.

23 Genesis 1:2.

24 Acts 2:1-4.

25 Genesis 2:7.

26 Ezekiel 37:10a.

27 Ezekiel 37:10b.

28 John 20:19-21.

29 This example comes from Ronald C. Greene, *The Spiritual Leadership of Disciples Elders: Leading the Church as Spiritual Community* (Claremont CA: Oikodome Publications, Disciples Seminary Foundation, 2003), 41.

30 For other forms of prayer see Chester P. Michael and Marie C. Norrisey, *Prayer and Temperament: Different Prayer Forms for Different Personality Types* (Charlottesville, VA: The Open Door, 1991) or Joseph D. Driskill, *Protestant Spiritual Exercises: Theology, History, Practice* (Harrisburg PA: Morehouse, 1999).

SPIRITUAL HABIT 2

31 David Whyte, "The Opening of Eyes," *Songs for Coming Home* (Langley, WA: Many Rivers Press, 1989).

32 Luke 24: 13-35.

33 Adapted from James E. Loder, *The Transforming Moment: Understanding Convictional Experiences* (San Francisco: Harper and Row, 1981), 3-4.

34 Loder, 101.

35 Sharon Parks, *The Critical Years: The Young Adult Search for a Faith to Live By*, (San Francisco: Harper and Row, 1986), 126.

36 Genesis 1:26a.

37 This understanding of the Christian way of life prevalent in the first two centuries was later reclaimed by teachers such as Abelard, Kant and Tillich. It stands in contrast to the doctrine generated in the third Century by Augustine

of Hippo which claims human beings are born in a state of sin and would be doomed to eternal damnation were it not for Jesus who died in their place, substituting his life for theirs in order to satisfy God's requirement of bloodshed.

38   George E. Ganss, S. J. translator and commentator, *The Spiritual Exercises of Saint Ignatius* (St. Louis: The Institute of Jesuit Sources, 1992), 33.

39   Ronald C. Greene defines Christianity Spirituality as "the exploration of our relationship with God in all life's dimensions, guided by the Spirit and centered on Jesus Christ, informed by the Scriptures, nourished by worship and study and service in the faith community, sustained by prayer, and expressed in ministry to our neighbors In the love of Jesus Christ." That integrated spirituality recognizes Christians experience God in their inner lives of the soul (the interpersonal dimension), in their relationships with people (the interpersonal dimension), in the systems of society (the structural dimension) and in creation (the environmental dimension) (See *The Spiritual Leadership of Disciples Elders*, 17, 20.) Greene first encountered those categories in a course entitled "Integrating Spirituality and Social Structures taught by John Mostyn, CFC at San Francisco Theological Seminary, San Anselmo, CA in January 1996. He subsequently used them to adapt Ignatius' Prayer of Examen for congregational purposes.

40   Charles Dickens, *A Christmas Carol* (London: Chapman and Hall, 1843).

SPIRITUAL HABIT 3

41   May Sarton, "Now I Become Myself," *Collected Poems* 1930-1993 (New York: W.W. Norton and Company, Inc., 1993).

42   Jean Piaget detailed how human brains develop the capacity for critical, abstract thinking in his work *The Psychology of the Child* (New York: Basic Books, 1969).

43.   Laurence Kohlberg, *The Psychology of Moral Development* (San Francisco: Harper and Row, 1984) and Carol Gilligan, *In a Different Voice: Psychological Theory and Women's Development* (Cambridge: MA: Harvard University Press, 1983).

44   Erik H. Erickson, *Identity: Youth and Crisis* (New York: W. W. Norton and Company, Inc., 1968).

45   James Fowler, John H. Westerhoff III, Thomas Merton, Steven Ivy, Don Edward Beck, Ken Wilber, Robert Kegan, and Elizabeth Liebert have written extensively about spiritual growth and development.

46   1 Corinthians 13:11.

47   Parker Palmer, *A Hidden Wholeness: The Journey Toward An Undivided Life* (San Francisco: John Wiley and Sons, 2004), 92.

48   Emily Dickenson "Tell the Truth But Tell It Slant," *Reading Edition* (Cambridge, MA: The Belknap Press of Harvard University, 1983).

49   Many transforming congregations have made particular use of resources from Living the Questions (http://www.livingthequestions.com) and Darkwood Brew (http://darkwoodbrew.org).

SPIRITUAL HABIT 4

50   *New and Selected Poems* (St. Paul, MN: Graywolf Press, 1998).
51   Genesis 1:6-7.
52   Genesis 1:11-25.
53   Psalm 78:25.
54   Exodus 16.
55   Mark 1:14b.
56   Matthew 5:3-6.
57   Mark 6:30-44, Matthew 14:13-21, Luke 9:10-17, John 6:1-13.
58   Isaiah 25:8, 1 Corinthians 15:54.
59   Romans 8:35-39.
60   Matthew 25:31-46.
61   2 Corinthians 6:19.
62   www.familypromise.org.
63   Luke 1:52-53.

SPIRITUAL HABIT 5

64   Martin Buber, *I and Thou*, Translated by Ronald Gregor Smith, (New York: Charles Scribners, 1958).
65   Luke 10:4.
66   John 16:13a.
67   John 14:26.
68   1 Corinthians 12:27.
69   Psalm 32:2, John 14:17, 16:13; 1 John 5:6.
70   1 Corinthians 2:15.
71   Zechariah 4:6.
72   Matthew 26:42.
73   For more suggestions about how to exegete your community, see Rick Morse, *From our Doorsteps: Developing a Ministry Plan that Makes Sense* (St. Louis: Chalice Press, 2010), 26-65.
74   Diana Butler Bass draws the distinction between the 20th Century Church that invited "joining" and the 21st Century Church that invites "joining in" *Christianity After Religion: The End of the Church and the Birth of a New Spiritual Awakening* (New York: HarperCollins, 2012), 205.

SPIRITUAL HABIT 6

75   Gloria Wade-Gayles ed. *My Soul is a Witness: African-American Women's Spirituality* (Boston: Beacon Press, 1995), 2.
76   Matthew 11:3, Luke 7:19.
77   Matthew 11:4-5, Luke 7:22.
78   John 14:25-26.
79   John 15:26-27.
80   Acts 4:18-20.
81   Hebrews 12:1a

SPIRITUAL HABIT 7

82   Henri J. M. Nouwen, *Reaching Out: The Three Movements of the Spiritual Life* (New York: Doubleday, 1975).
83   Kinnaman and Lyons, 181-197.
84   Two out of three faith communities in 2010 had experienced a high level of conflict over worship, finances, leadership and/or church priorities. Those conflicted faith communities declined in worship attendance twice as fast as other churches who were not going through conflict. Conflict has a corrosive effect on church vitality. David A. Roozen, "A Decade of Change In American Faith Communities 2000-2010," *Faith Communities Today Project*, Hartford Institute for Religion Research, (Hartford Seminary, 2011).
85   Jerome Murphy-O'Connor, *St. Paul's Corinth* (Wilmington, DE: Michael Glazier, 1983), 156, 158.
86   The custom is described in 1 Corinthians 8:10.
87   See 1 Corinthians. 13:30.
88   Pliny, "Letters," 2:6.
89   1 Corinthians 6:15. In contrast to Paul, the anonymous author of *The Epistle of Mathetes to Diognetus* (vi) understood the role of Christians, not as the body itself, but as the *soul* of the body. To put it simply: What the soul is in the body, Christians are in the world. The soul is dispersed through all the members of the body, and the Christians are scattered through all the cities of the world. The soul dwells in the world but does not belong to the world.... The soul is shut up in the body, and yet itself holds the body together; while Christians are retained in the world as in a prison, and yet themselves hold the world together.
90   People from all economic strata, as well as Gentiles and Jews, ate together (Acts 11:2-3).
91   Halvor Moxnes, "Patron-Client Relations and the New Community in Luke-Acts," in *The Social World of Luke-Acts* (Peabody, MA: Hendrickson Publishing, 1991), 242, 244-50.
92   Plutarch, "Dinner of the Seven Wise Men," in *Moralia*, vol. 2, trans. Frank Cole Babbitt, Loeb Classical Library (Cambridge: Harvard University Press,

1956), 148A-149F. In this fictional story, Plutarch discusses the custom of ranking when one of the characters expresses insult at the position offered. He also cites examples of ranking in "Table Talk," *Moralia*, vol. 3, 616A-617B. The ranking of guests is also described at the banquet of Agathon in Plato, "Symposium," 177A-E.

93 Moxnes, "Patron-Client," 245.

94 Jerome H. Neyrey, "The Idea of Purity in Mark's Gospel" *Semeia* #35, Society of Biblical Literature, Scholars' Press, 1986, 95.

95 Neyrey, 95-98.

96 Mark 3:23-28.

97 Gilbert R. Rendle refers to behavioral covenants as "Holy Manners" in his book *Leading Change in the Congregation: Spiritual and Organizational Tools for Leaders* (Bethesda, MD: Alban Institute, 1999). The Center for Courage and Renewal refers to behavior covenants as "Boundary Markers" and they utilize them in each Circle of Trust they develop.

98 This is a practice of the Taize community where people from many different faith traditions gather.

SPIRITUAL HABIT 8

99 Bass, 21.

100 Bass, 77-81.

101 These four reasons given for growing indifference toward church are named studies which already have been cited above (ARIS and the Barna Group project called "Faith that Lasts" reported out in the book *UnChristian*). Earlier studies which foreshadowed the current mass exodus from the church were Wade Clark Roof's *Spiritual Marketplace: Baby Boomers and the Remaking of American Religion* (Princeton, NJ: Princeton University Press, 1999) and Robert Wuthnow's *After Heaven: Spirituality in America Since the 1950s* (Berkeley: University of California Press, 1998).

102 Bass, 20.

103 Robert C. Fuller, *Spiritual, But Not Religious: Understanding Unchurched America* (New York: Oxford University Press, 2001) 4.

104 Robert Wuthnow, *The Restructuring of American Religion* (Princeton: Princeton University Press, 1988), 73f.

105 The patristic fathers put forth the *"Christus Victor theory of atonement"* in which Christ conquers Satan and the evil powers to free humanity from the bondage of death. Irenaeus and Origen put forth the "ransom theory of atonement" in which Christ paid Satan's price in order to free humanity from the bonds of sin and death and to bind Satan's power. Anselm put forth the "satisfaction theory of atonement" in which God demanded the sacrifice of a perfect human being to satisfy justice. Abelard put forth the "subjective view of atonement" in which God loved humanity so deeply that he sent his son to die

so that humans could find their way back home, living as children made in the image of God. Process theologians understand the atonement as God becoming incarnate in order to swallow up death so that all human experience is now in Christ and death no longer can harm humans. For a concise discussion of various theories of what "Christ died for us" means see Ronald E. Heine, *Classical Christian Doctrine* (Grand Rapids, MI: Baker Academic, 2013), 116-127.

106 Gresham Machen,*Christianity and Liberalism* (Trustees u/w J. Gresham Machen, 1923), 106-108, 158-60, 172-73.

107 Kate Bowler, *Blessed: A History of the American Prosperity Gospel* (New York: Oxford University Press, 2013).

108 Bruce Wilkinson and David Knopp, *The Prayer of Jabez: Breaking Through To the Blessed Life* (Colorado Springs: Multnomah Books, 2000).

109 The prayer of Jabez found in 1 Chronicles 4:10.

110 Joel Osteen, *Your Best Life Now: Seven Steps to Living at Your Full Potential* (Nashville: FaithWords, 2004).

111 ARIS study, 2009.

112 Steven Pinker, *The Better Angels of Our Nature* (New York: Penguin Group, 2011).

113 See Robert Lane, *The Loss of Happiness in Market Democracies* (New Haven: Yale University Press, 2000) and Gregg Easterbrook, *The Progress Paradox: How Life Gets Better While People Feel Worse* (New York: Random House, 2004).

114 Matthew 13:52b.

SPIRITUAL HABIT 9

115 Caroline Myss, PhD, *Anatomy of the Spirit: The Seven Stages of Power and Healing* (New York: Harmony Books, 1996), 208.

116 John 5:2-9.

117 Myss, 211-212.

118 1 Corinthians 12:26.

119 For a more complete discussion of how systems work see Murray Bowen, *Family Theory in Clinical Practice* (Northvale, NJ: Jason Aronson, 1978, 1985), Edwin H Friedman, *A Failure of Nerve: Leadership in the Age of the Quick Fix* (Bethesda, MD: Friedman Estate, 1999), and Peter L. Steinke, *Congregational Leadership in Anxious Times: Being Calm and Courageous No Matter What* (Herndon, VA: The Alban Institute, 2006).

SPIRITUAL HABIT 10

120 Wendell Berry, "The Wild Geese" from *The Country of Marriage* (Wendell Berry, 1973).

121 C.S. Lewis, *The Last Battle* (New York: Collier Books, 1956), 144-148.

122 Dorothy Sayers, "The Other Six Deadly Sins: An Address Given to the Public Morality Council at Coxton Hall, Westminster, on October 23, 1941."

123 Tony Dokoupil, "Is The Onslaught Making Us Crazy?" *Newsweek:* July 16, 2012, 27.

124 Juliet B. Schor, *Born to Buy: The Commercialized Child and the New Consumer Culture* (New York: Scribner, 2004), 10.

SPIRITUAL HABIT 11

125 Parker Palmer, *A Hidden Wholeness: The Journey Toward An Undivided Life* (San Francisco: John Wiley and Sons, 2004), 26.

SPIRITUAL HABIT 12

126 Vaclav Havel, "It Is I Who Must Begin" from *Letters to Olga* (New York: Alfred A. Knof, 1988).

127 I first heard this analogy from Alan Roxburg at a conference in Idaho in 2003.

128 Patrick Overton is credited of writing this in a poem called "Faith," although some form of it likely existed in the Celtic Oral tradition long before he re-appropriated it.

129 Acts 15:1-4.

130 Acts15:5-11.

131 Acts15:12.

132 Acts15:13-21.

133 Acts 15:22-32.

134 This story was told in Ruth Fletcher, *Take, Break, and Receive: The Process of Discernment in the Christian Church (Disciples of Christ)*, (Indianapolis: Homeland Ministries, 1999), 32-33.

135 Jeremiah 32:1-44.

FRESH EXPRESSIONS

136 Wendell Berry, "The Real Work," *Collected Poems* (Berkeley, CA: Counterpoint, 1987).

A CHURCH THAT MATTERS

137 Thomas Merton, *New Seeds of Contemplation* (Boston: Shambhala Publications, 2003), 148.

138 Matthew 13:1-9.

139 See Deuteronomy 30:19.

140 This movement corresponds with the first stage of change described in C. Otto Scharmer's *U Theory: Leading from the Future as it Emerges* (San Francisco: Berrett-Koehler, 2009).

141 Scharmer. These questions move the group into the fourth stage of change called Co-Creating.

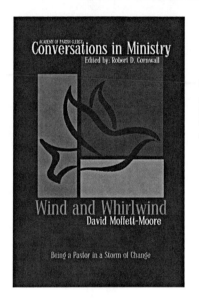
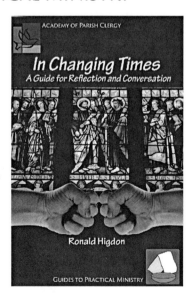

More from Energion Publications

Personal Study

Holy Smoke! Unholy Fire	Bob McKibben	$14.99
The Jesus Paradigm	David Alan Black	$17.99
When People Speak for God	Henry Neufeld	$17.99
The Sacred Journey	Chris Surber	$11.99

Christian Living

It's All Greek to Me	David Alan Black	$3.99
Grief: Finding the Candle of Light	Jody Neufeld	$8.99
My Life Story	Becky Lynn Black	$14.99
Crossing the Street	Robert LaRochelle	$16.99
Life as Pilgrimage	David Moffett-Moore	14.99

Bible Study

Learning and Living Scripture	Lentz/Neufeld	$12.99
From Inspiration to Understanding	Edward W. H. Vick	$24.99
Philippians: A Participatory Study Guide	Bruce Epperly	$9.99
Ephesians: A Participatory Study Guide	Robert D. Cornwall	$9.99
Ecclesiastes: A Participatory Study Guide	Russell Meek	$9.99

Theology

Creation in Scripture	Herold Weiss	$12.99
Creation: the Christian Doctrine	Edward W. H. Vick	$12.99
The Politics of Witness	Allan R. Bevere	$9.99
Ultimate Allegiance	Robert D. Cornwall	$9.99
History and Christian Faith	Edward W. H. Vick	$9.99
The Journey to the Undiscovered Country	William Powell Tuck	$9.99
Process Theology	Bruce G. Epperly	$4.99

Ministry

Clergy Table Talk	Kent Ira Groff	$9.99
Out of This World	Darren McClellan	$24.99

Generous Quantity Discounts Available
Dealer Inquiries Welcome
Energion Publications — P.O. Box 841
Gonzalez, FL 32560
Website: http://energionpubs.com
Phone: (850) 525-3916

CPSIA information can be obtained
at www.ICGtesting.com
Printed in the USA
FSOW02n0157210616
21791FS

9 781631 992070